NEW DIRECTIONS FOR COMMUNITY COLLEGES

Arthur M. Cohen
EDITOR-IN-CHIEF

Florence B. Brawer
ASSOCIATE EDITOR

Developing International Education Programs

Richard K. Greenfield
College Consortium for International Studies

EDITOR

Number 70, Summer 1990

JOSSEY-BASS INC., PUBLISHERS
San Francisco • Oxford

EDUCATIONAL RESOURCES INFORMATION CENTER

Clearinghouse For Junior Colleges

UNIVERSITY OF CALIFORNIA, LOS ANGELES

Developing International Education Programs.
Richard K. Greenfield (ed.).
New Directions for Community Colleges, no. 70.
Volume XVIII, number 2.

NEW DIRECTIONS FOR COMMUNITY COLLEGES
Arthur M. Cohen, Editor-in-Chief
Florence B. Brawer, Associate Editor

NEW DIRECTIONS FOR COMMUNITY COLLEGES is part of The Jossey-Bass Higher Education Series and is published quarterly by Jossey-Bass Inc., Publishers (publication number USPS 121-710) in association with the ERIC Clearinghouse for Junior Colleges. Second-class postage paid at San Francisco, California, and at additional mailing offices. Postmaster: Send address changes to Jossey-Bass Inc., Publishers, 350 Sansome Street, San Francisco, California 94104.

THE MATERIAL in this publication is based on work sponsored wholly or in part by the Office of Educational Research and Improvement, U.S. Department of Education, under contract number RI-88-062002. Its contents do not necessarily reflect the views of the Department, or any other agency of the U.S. Government.

EDITORIAL CORRESPONDENCE should be sent to the Editor-in-Chief, Arthur M. Cohen, at the ERIC Clearinghouse for Junior Colleges, University of California, Los Angeles, California 90024.

Library of Congress Catalog Card Number LC 85-644753

International Standard Serial Number ISSN 0194-3081

International Standard Book Number ISBN 1-55542-823-1

Cover photograph by Rene Sheret, Los Angeles, California © 1990.

Manufactured in the United States of America. Printed on acid-free paper.

CONTENTS

EDITOR'S NOTES

The accelerating pace of technological and economic change is continuing to shrink our world at a rate that is difficult for most of us to comprehend. Relative ease of travel and near-instantaneous world telecommunication systems, coupled with the development of an interdependent world economy, have heightened an awareness of the need for political accommodation based on mutual appreciation of political, linguistic, and social differences. In turn, these developments have challenged our educational systems to adapt to a "one-world" environment.

Despite the reality of world interdependence, it is extremely difficult for the average person to think in global terms, since so much of life experience is localized. Similarly, community colleges have been concentrating on delivering services to meet the needs of local or regional communities for decades. This localized strength of the typical community college is also a weakness, because sometimes it stands as a psychological barrier to expanding the horizons of sponsoring communities' leadership groups as well as those of trustees, staff, and students. Continuing to stress service in response to local needs, in the face of the need for flexibility, population mobility, and world economic, ecological, and political interdependence, will be counterproductive in the long run. Today, our "village" is truly global in a very real sense.

The experience of studying abroad is no longer confined to the privileged few in elite, private institutions in the United States. Today, study abroad is only one aspect of a multidimensional effort on the part of many public and private colleges and community colleges to internationalize the curriculum. Most practitioners in the field of international education agree that the level of interest and attention to various facets of study abroad, student- and faculty-exchanges with non-American institutions, foreign technical assistance programs, reception of foreign students, and intercultural education has expanded at an accelerating pace during the last two decades. Despite this heightened interest and activity, there is little "hard data" being collected on a systematic basis, either by colleges or by governmental agencies.

In its recent report, *Building Communities: A Vision for a New Century*, the American Association of Community and Junior Colleges' Commission on the Future of Community Colleges expressed great concern over the shocking ignorance of the great majority of Americans with respect to the heritage of other nations and the reality of an interdependent world (Commission on the Future of Community Colleges, 1988). Therefore, it urged that the general education sequence in community colleges provide students with a better understanding of other cultures.

Currently community colleges may be involved in one or more of any of these facets of international or intercultural education:

- Semester, intersession, or summer student study-abroad programs
- Mini-study tours
- Student-exchange programs
- Faculty-exchange programs
- Organized support programs for foreign students on campus
- English as a Second Language programs
- Intercultural and area-studies courses and programs
- Internationalizing liberal arts, humanities, and business curricula
- Campus-community program activities with an international emphasis
- Consultation or support services for foreign institutions or countries, particularly in developing technical programs or community-college counterparts
- Facilitating staff participation in overseas professional development seminars and
- Participation in regional, state, and national consortia focused on international education.

From an institutional point of view, study-abroad programs are not moneymakers—indeed, they cost more than they earn, in terms of administrative and support staff time, travel, and so forth, but such programs may attract better students, use the entrepreneurial drives of some faculty members, enhance the employability of the students involved, lead to interinstitutional linkages, and provide opportunities for institutional and staff renewal. Perhaps the overriding issue is a philosophical one—can the community college's mission be attuned to reality if it ignores the international factor in today's world?

Community colleges are faced with a bewildering range of possible activities in international education. An almost paralyzing set of choices faces colleges even within the obvious and traditional activity of study-abroad programs. Added to normal concerns over diffusion of mission, immediate and long-range costs, and staffing, is the possibility of adverse local or state reaction to the concept of community college involvement in programs attuned to more than the perceived local, regional, or national needs. Hence, while some community colleges have become active in international education in a well-planned, adequately staffed, and soundly funded way, many more have paid mere lip service to such ideas rather than make a sustained commitment.

For any community college or district to have a viable and effective international education program, regardless of affiliation with a consortium, it needs the following:

- A strong commitment by the president and key academic leaders and interested faculty
- A commitment from the board of trustees via a supportive policy statement
- Inclusion of international education in the mission-and-goals statement of the college
- A process for ongoing involvement of interested faculty and staff
- An adequate structure to administer or coordinate programs and resources with qualified, knowledgeable personnel. A full-time director of international education, or at least a faculty member with substantial released time, a clearly visible office, and clerical support, are absolutely necessary, as are funds for publicity, program development, and travel. This is true even if the college is part of a consortium and does not attempt to launch its own programs.
- A good public information system to keep the college and community aware of the program and its activities
- Participation by community advisory and support groups.

There is a special challenge for community colleges and small to moderate-sized public and private baccalaureate degree-granting institutions in trying to move from rhetoric and general interest to a practical, effective international education program that is available to more than a few students or an occasional faculty member. In this book, various authors touch on some of the ways in which such institutions may be able to develop reasonably effective programs, including the consortial approach, without having to "reinvent the wheel." Unfortunately, space limitations make it impossible to cover every aspect of international education or to examine any one approach in depth. However, the authors hope that their efforts will assist others in their search for more effective education in our increasingly integrated world.

Richard K. Greenfield
Editor

Reference

Commission on the Future of Community Colleges. *Building Communities: A Vision for a New Century*. Washington, D.C.: American Association of Community and Junior Colleges, 1988. (ED 293 578)

Richard K. Greenfield is executive director of the College Consortium for International Studies. He has served as chancellor of the St. Louis Community College and as founding president of two community colleges.

Community colleges are viewed as newcomers in the field of international education, but they are playing an increasing role in the search for world understanding.

Lessons from the Past in Developing International Education in Community Colleges

David G. Scanlon

The classic definition of international education is that it "is a term used to describe the various educational and cultural relations among nations" (Scanlon, 1960, p. 1). Originally the phrase was used to describe formal education, but today the concept of international education has been broadened to include government relations programs, promotion of mutual understanding between nations, educational assistance to underdeveloped regions, cross-cultural education, and international communications.

To understand the development of international education in the community colleges of the United States it is necessary to place it within the historical framework of the United States as well as the world. The interaction of world history, U.S. history, and specifically the history of higher education, accounts for the current position of international education in the community colleges.

The phenomenon of international education is actually as old as nations themselves. One finds the same concepts as those given at the beginning of this essay in the writings of Comenius, Montaigne, Rousseau, Kant, Fichte, Penn, and numerous other scholars and philosophers. It appears that after every major war from the seventeenth century onward, there has been a determined constituency that called for nations to work together for peace. The outline for the present United Nations Educational, Scientific, and Cultural Organization (UNESCO) can be found in the writings of Marc-Antoine Jullien (1817), who wrote in the period following the Napoleonic wars. Recent proposals for the Erasmus Project, to be part of

NEW DIRECTIONS FOR COMMUNITY COLLEGES, no. 70, Summer 1990 © Jossey-Bass Inc., Publishers the emerging European Economic Community, can be found in the writings of Herman Molkenboer, a Dutch lawyer who wrote after the Franco-Prussian War (Molkenboer, 1891). During the same period, John Eaton, U.S. Commissioner of Education, had presented to the International Conference on Education, held in Philadelphia in 1876, a plan for a permanent organization that would be responsible for future international conferences and be a source for the exchange of information about education (Department of the Interior, 1877).

However, it was in the post–World War I period that international education assumed a more visible character. Improved transportation and communication had brought the world closer together than it had ever been before. The Committee for International Cooperation and the International Bureau of Education were created.

It was also in the post–World War I period that international education began to become more visible in American higher education. For the first time, American four-year-college students began spending a semester abroad. This was an important step forward in that such study abroad was viewed as a legitimate part of a four-year program with rigid academic requirements.

On local campuses during the interwar period there were some foreign-area study programs, but they were very limited and were often taught by the "mish kids," the sons and daughters of missionaries. These were among the few who had lived in foreign cultures, particularly nonwestern societies, and knew their languages. In many cases their contributions to area studies were outstanding, for example, Henry O. Reischauer.

Robert B. Hall (1974), who worked with the Ethnographic Board during World War II preparing a list of Americans who were foreign-area specialists, wrote, "For all practical purposes there were no trained specialists at the outbreak of the war" (p. 2). This was particularly evident in the areas of Africa, the Middle East, and Asia. Hall suggested that during the war our military and diplomatic ability had increased markedly, but our intellectual preparation, our knowledge of the nonwestern world, would continue to be virtually nonexistent.

If the government and the universities lacked specialists with a knowledge of foreign cultures and languages, there was a corresponding lack of information on the part of the general public. Thomas A. Bailey, a Stanford University diplomatic historian, wrote in his study, *The Man in the Street: The Impact of American Public Opinion on Foreign Policy,* that ignorance of foreign policy could be correlated with prejudice, susceptibility to propaganda, and chauvinism. Bailey argued that "a well-informed citizenry is as important as battleships" (1948, p. 151).

In 1940, it is estimated, there were 150,000 academics in higher education. Fewer than 200 could be considered to be in the field of international studies. It is difficult to realize today, but in the period immediately following World War II there were no journals for academics to communicate with each other in area studies, and the few specialists in the universities were isolated—there were no area associations where specialists could meet and exchange common ideas and information. The author recalls a meeting in Philadelphia in the 1950s at which a handful of scholars started the African Studies Association. The Asian Studies Association was not started until the 1960s.

In 1946 Congress passed the Fulbright Act, which opened the door for Americans to increase their knowledge by studying abroad. The first global and educational exchange program, the Smith-Mundt Act, was put into effect in 1949. The Act specifically stated that in order "to promote a better understanding of the U.S. and to promote mutual understanding among all people, there shall be an educational exchange service to cooperate with nations in (a) the interchange of persons; (b) the rendering of technical and other services; (c) the interchange of developments in the field of education, and the arts and sciences."

For the next twenty years government and private agencies made a tremendous effort to expand and develop international studies. Unfortunately, the community colleges were not included in this effort to broaden America's perspective of the world.

There has never been such a national interest in international education as during the period from 1959 to 1969. The large grants made by the government during this period to colleges and universities, unfortunately, did not include community colleges. This money permitted institutions to establish area-study centers and engage in technical assistance abroad. The exclusion of the community colleges was indeed unfortunate. A major study of government interest in international education, *Government Programs in International Education (A Survey and Hand Book)*, published in 1959, makes no reference to community colleges although the purpose of the study is to show the need to internationalize campuses.

A second major publication by the U.S. government, *International Education: Past, Present, Problems and Prospects* was prepared by the Task Force on International Education, chaired by John Brademas, and published in 1966. To be sure, a few contracts to community colleges and technical institutes were awarded by the Agency for International Development in the 1960s, but they were the exception to the rule of working with four-year colleges and universities.

It was also during the 1960s that consciousness by the United States of world affairs was increased by the establishment of the Peace Corps. There were few communities that did not have some young man or woman from its area join the Peace Corps. The ensuing publicity helped members of the community concentrate on one area of the world. More people learned about third-world countries than ever before. Peace Corps volunteers were from the local community and, upon their return, were interpreters of the foreign culture for their area.

If the 1960s represented a bleak picture for international education in the community colleges, this may well have been because the community college movement was virtually sweeping the country during this period. To build, organize, and administer a new college was a primary responsibility. In many cases there was little time left to think about international education.

In addition, there were some who argued that international education was not the responsibility of the community college. The concept of the "community" was defined by some in very narrow, parochial terms. Others argued that the needs of the neighborhood were bound inextricably to the realities of the international community.

By the 1970s the surge of interest in international education had declined rapidly. The government funds that were so supportive in the 1960s were reduced drastically. The foundations that had played a major role in the expansion of international studies in the 1960s turned their interest elsewhere. The Peace Corps was reduced to a shadow of its former self. The divisiveness caused by the Vietnam War and by economic inflation were having a debilitating effect on the country.

Despite these problems, there was a growing sense in many community college educators that community colleges had to expand their interest from the "neighborhood" to the world. In retrospect, it is remarkable to see the growth of international education in the community colleges during the 1970s despite the difficult problems of finance.

The Central Administration of the State University of New York asked Rockland Community College to establish an office of international education in 1969. "The idea of 'internationalizing' a community college was a new and radical idea at the time since most attempts along these lines had been clearly reserved for four-year colleges and university centers, mostly the so-called junior year abroad program" (Hess, 1976, p. 5). By 1975 Rockland had (1) developed international and comparative analysis within traditional disciplines, (2) developed and expanded language and civilization offerings in scheduled classes, and (3) provided overseas study opportunities.

Foreign Students

The year 1975 also found over 50,000 foreign students, representing one-third of all foreign students in the United States, in community colleges. In nine years the number of reported foreign students in community colleges had increased 1,000 percent. By 1976 more than 60,000 foreign students were studying in community colleges in this country (Hess, 1976).

In 1977, the National Association of Foreign Student Affairs (NAFSA) and the American Association of Community and Junior Colleges (AACJC) formed a joint liaison committee to formally focus their interest and energies on programs and activities in international exchange. As a result of this liaison a colloquium was held at Wingspread, Racine, Wisconsin, in October 1977, dealing with the foreign student on community college campuses. The formal topic was "The Foreign Student in the United States Community and Junior Colleges," and the colloquium represented a milestone in reviewing the presence of foreign students in the community colleges.

It was difficult to count the number of foreign students in community colleges in the United States until the 1960s. Previously, the few students who had come to the United States had attended private two-year institutions. By the 1970s, many third-world politicians and educators realized that the varied and comprehensive programs offered by the community colleges were exactly what their countries needed. Unfortunately, this occurred at the same time that the U.S. government was making severe reductions in foreign aid and, therefore, foreign student aid was cut drastically.

A 1967 study of foreign students reported that (a) community colleges enrolled few foreign students, (b) community colleges that did enroll foreign students were most likely to be in California, Michigan, or Illinois, (c) most foreign students were full-time and enrolled in a transfer program, and (d) most community colleges accepted foreign students but did not recruit them.

In 1974 the Community/Junior College Committee of NAFSA sponsored a survey of all two-year institutions. The committee reported about 50,000 foreign students in community and junior colleges in 1973-1974. In 1976-1977 a follow-up study with 356 community and junior colleges reported 20,794 foreign students.

While this appeared to be a substantial drop, the new figure probably was due to changes in the definition of a foreign student. In 1974, the NAFSA study counted as foreign students holders of visas, refugees, and immigrants. In 1977, surveys included only visa holders and refugees. Immigrants were not included, hence the wide disparity between the figures.

An important study of foreign students in U.S. community colleges in 1976-1977 by Thomas Diener found that among foreign students in U.S. community and junior colleges (1) most foreign students (66 percent) were full-time, (2) 47 percent were in the United States on nonresident visas, 38 percent were refugees, and (3) 52 percent paid their bills with money from home, 14 percent with money in the United States, 11 percent from home governments, and 3 percent from payment received for campus employment (Diener, 1977).

William G. Shannon published *A Survey of International Intercultural Education in Two Year Colleges—1976* (1978). The purpose of the study, which collected data from 200 colleges, was to "identify international/intercultural programs and activities of community, junior and technical colleges, to encourage replication and to suggest how such services can be strengthened in the future" (p. 5).

Shannon pointed out that there is little doubt that the inclusion of two-year colleges under Title VI—Foreign Studies and Language Development greatly expanded the opportunities for community colleges to participate in international education. When originally passed in 1958, Title VI had been restricted to four-year colleges and universities. However, in the 1970s, due to the work of AACJC and other educational organizations, a new section, 603, was added, which permitted two-year institutions to apply for and receive grants.

His study also showed the value of and potential for ties between community colleges and the international business community and links between two-year colleges and four-year colleges and universities. In both regards Shannon was predicting what would become common practice by the late 1980s.

International Education Consortia

While there is ample evidence to illustrate the growing interest in international education in community colleges, there is no doubt that the establishment of three consortia contributed markedly to its development.

International/Intercultural Committee of AACJC. AACJC established an office of international programs in 1971. The very creation of the office indicated rising early interest in the field. Increasing demands led to the establishment of the International/Intercultural Committee (I/IC) in 1976. Sixty colleges formed the core membership. Today, one hundred institutions are members. In addition to serving as a valuable clearinghouse for information on international education of interest to community colleges, the I/IC provides a valuable link to U.S. government offices and foreign governments and has helped numerous colleges start an international education program on their campuses.

College Consortium for International Studies. In 1973, a Tri-State Consortium on international education was formed with Mercer Community College (N.J.), Harrisburg Community College (Pa.), and Rockland Community College (N.Y.). This pioneer work became a model for other areas of the country where community colleges were interested in study-abroad programs for their students. While the semester-abroad concept had been in existence since the close of World War I, it was always assumed that the semester would be taken in the junior year and would be in the liberal arts. This new consortium provided study-abroad programs for students who might be terminating their education in the community college. There would be no "junior" year. Moreover, the new consortium, while offering the traditional liberal arts abroad, reflected the comprehensive nature of the community college and offered opportunities for students in career areas as well. Students in business, law enforcement, health services, and a variety of other areas were welcomed into the program, and a program abroad was found for them.

The Tri-State Consortium evolved into the College Consortium for International Studies (CCIS) in 1975. Today, over 150 campuses are members, and CCIS has broadened its educational base to include a significant number of public and private four-year colleges and universities. It sends approximately 1,100 students abroad for a semester. Programs have been established in eighteen countries—Europe, the Middle East, and Asia. All overseas programs are carefully supervised to maintain high quality.

Community Colleges for International Development. The College Consortium for International Development (CCID) was founded in 1976. While I/IC of AACJC tends to be interested in all areas of international education and CCIS's main concern is study abroad, Community Colleges for International Development has focused its concern on bilateral agreements that provide technical assistance to other countries. CCID was organized with six community colleges and has purposely kept its membership small. Today there are thirteen member institutions (one in Canada) and twenty-three affiliated colleges (including two in Canada). The objectives of CCID today are to provide (1) assistance to countries in mid-level manpower training and technical and vocational education, (2) opportunities for international study, exchange, and professional development for students and faculty of U.S. community colleges and cooperating institutions abroad, and (3) leadership and services in the development of international education in community colleges.

State, Country, Regional, and Service Consortia. In addition to these national consortia there are now many state consortia in international education—California, Florida, Illinois, Michigan, Minnesota, and New Jersey. In other cases regional organizations have been formed, such as the Northwest Consortium. Still others are organized by relationship to a country. An example of this type is the American-Chinese Educational Consortium for Academic and Technical Exchange, formed in 1987 to help foster exchange and sister-college programs between institutions of higher education in the People's Republic of China and U.S. community colleges. Some cities, such as Los Angeles, are large enough to have their own international education program and have developed an enthusiastic interest in international education.

Numerous other types of organizations have arisen that provide a variety of educational experiences for community college students. Partnership in Service Learning offers community college students the opportunity to participate in overseas social projects. The students, with a mentor, design a program for which they receive academic credit.

The Role of the Community College in International Education in the United States. While dramatic developments were taking place in the 1970s, it was not until the close of the decade that the U.S. government recognized the crucial role community colleges play in this important area. To be sure, some federal grants had been available previously but never before had community colleges been recognized as playing a crucial role. *Strength Through Wisdom: A Critique of U.S. Capability* was published in 1979 (Perkins, 1979). The subtitle is *A Report to the President from the President's Commission on Foreign Languages and International Studies.* The report stressed the political, economic, and social need for international education. It pointed out that "international education is an important prerequisite for national security" (pp. 1–2). The report warns that a nation's welfare depends in large measure on the intellectual and psychological strengths that are derived from a perceptive vision of the world beyond its own borders.

Strength Through Wisdom is one of the three most important U.S. government publications on international education. The others are the previously mentioned *Government Programs in International Education* (1959) and *International Education: Past, Present, Problems and Prospects* (1966). However, in the two earlier reports no attention was given to the community colleges. In *Strength Through Wisdom* the important role of the community college is recognized; in fact, this book views the community college as a crucial institution if the United States hopes to reach international literacy. For many students the community college is going to be the place where they are introduced to world cultures and societies. In addition, the Commission pointed out, community colleges were enrolling half the adults enrolled in credit and noncredit continuing education programs. They are truly "community" educators.

In 1980, another important study of international education was prepared for the Carnegie Council on Policy Studies by Dr. Barbara Burn. Entitled *Expanding the International Dimension of Higher Education,* the study is a comprehensive review of international education in higher educational institutions and, unlike other studies, includes the community colleges (Burn, 1980). Burn stresses the role of the community college as a crucial element if internationalization is to be truly effective, noting that

> The extent to which community colleges are internationalized is important in assessing the current state of international education, because one-third of all degree-credit students in higher education attend community colleges and over 50 percent of first year students enter these colleges [p. 23].

By the early 1980s, studies were also appearing that provided excellent guidelines and examples for colleges interested in developing international education on their campuses. Two excellent examples of this type of publication are *The Community College and International Education: A Report of Progress*, by Seymour Fersh and Edward Fitchen (1981), and a follow-up study, *The Community College and International Education*, Volume 2, by Seymour Fersh and William Greene (1984).

International Education and International Business. Throughout the 1980s, international education expanded rapidly on community college campuses: The I/IC of AACJC now has over one hundred members; CCIS has increased from 30 campuses to 150 campuses; CCID has expanded its membership and overseas activities. Community colleges have established "sister" relationships with colleges in Latin America, Europe, and Asia. Technical assistance, once viewed as the monopoly of the four-year college and university, is now being offered by numerous community colleges. Efforts to internationalize the curriculum are now common on many campuses.

With activities expanding dramatically, the theme of international education and international business has dominated much of the 1980s, particularly in the past few years. As the global technological revolution has taken place, it has become evident that if the United States is to maintain its industrial prominence, it must know more about other cultures and their languages than it has demonstrated hitherto.

The Florida legislature was among the first to recognize the interrelationship of international education and international business. The legislature directed the Department of Education in consultation with the Department of Commerce to study the state's activities and future needs related to international education, ". . . particularly those aimed at promoting trade and business" (Fersh and Greene, 1984, p. 101).

Some community colleges responded to the challenge on the national scene and have established comprehensive business programs. Lynda Icochea, director of the Center for International Studies at Bergen Community College, established an International Trade Round Table Association in New Jersey to assist local industry in functioning more adequately in the international marketplace. The Round Table, composed of local business people involved in international trade or interested in becoming involved, meets regularly at the college. Started in 1980, the Round Table has consistently expanded (Icochea, 1984).

The relationship of business to international education has been recognized and emphasized by the I/IC of AACJC both in annual meetings and in publications. Two outstanding publications by AACJC are *International Trade Education: Issues and Programs*, edited by James R. Mahoney and Clyde Sakamoto (1985), and *The Next Challenge: Balancing International Competition and Cooperation*, edited by Clyde Sakamoto and Mary Fifield (1987). In the last few years, demands for international education as a necessary component of international business have been made on the federal, state, and regional level. Demands have been made that all levels of the educational ladder be internationalized.

The Southern Governors' Association (1986) published *Cornerstone of Competition: International Education,* a report arguing that only recently has the business community come to the realization that we operate in a global economy. The report continues:

> Tomorrow is not our only problem. Each day exacts a political and economic price for our inability to understand and to communicate with our global neighbors. If business and government leaders are not prepared to participate in today's world it may not matter how well we prepare for tomorrow [p. 7].

In 1987, the National Governors' Association published *Making America Work: Productive People, Productive Policies.* The report warns that the once-predictable international marketplace has been transformed into an interdependent and rapidly changing market. All regions of the United States are caught up in fierce competition for jobs, resources, and markets. Workers have found that their very jobs can be at stake because of fluctuating exchange rates or, in some cases, because employers have not kept up with the latest technology. Farmers find themselves facing falling foreign demand and failing commodity prices.

At the 1989 winter meeting of the National Governors' Conference, a panel of governors warned that the economic well-being of the United States was in jeopardy because too many Americans are ignorant of the language and cultures of other nations. Governor Gerald L. Baliles of Virginia indicated we are not well prepared for international trade. Governor Thomas H. Kean of New Jersey said that without international training in international studies Americans will be out-competed in the world market (National Governors' Association, 1987).

The thrust of all the reports cited above suggests that while the study of international business itself needs to be rapidly expanded, the success of the United States in the world market will only be achieved if all of its citizens are well informed in world affairs. This means that international studies and the study of foreign languages are the concern of all students and all citizens.

Conclusion

Today we see the convergence of three interest groups in the development and expansion of international education. First, there are the traditional supporters who, ever since Comenius, have believed that international education, that understanding other cultures and languages, would contribute to the elimination of war and would build world peace. Second, there are those who view international education as a pragmatic tool necessary for national security. This view developed in the post-World War II period. Finally, we now see international education as a prime prerequisite for international trade and for maintaining our standard of living.

As a result of these interests we can expect to see the expansion of international education on all levels of the educational ladder. However, the particular role of the community college in U.S. society suggests that it will play a crucial role in this development.

References

American Association of Community and Junior Colleges, and the National Liaison Committee of Foreign Student Admissions. *The Foreign Student in the United States Community and Junior Colleges: A Colloquium Held at Wingspread, Racine, Wisconsin, October 18-20, 1977.* New York: College Entrance Examination Board, 1978. (ED 154 858)

American Council on Education. *Fact Book on Higher Education, 1984-1985.* New York: Macmillan, 1986.

Bailey, T. A. *The Man in the Street: The Impact of American Public Opinion on Foreign Policy.* New York: Macmillan, 1948.

Burn, B.B. *Expanding the International Dimension of Higher Education.* San Francisco: Jossey-Bass, 1980. (ED 183 117)

Deiner, T. "Profile of Foreign Students in the U.S. Community and Junior College." In *The Foreign Student in the United States Community and Junior Colleges: A Colloquium Held at Wingspread, Racine, Wisconsin, October 18-20, 1977.* New York: College Entrance Examination Board, 1978.

Department of the Interior, Bureau of Education. *The International Conference on Education Held at Philadelphia, July 17, in Connection with the International Exhibition of 1876.* Washington, D.C.: U.S. Government Printing Office, 1877, pp. 84-89.

Fersh, S., and Fitchen, E. (eds.). *The Community College and International Education: A Report of Progress.* Cocoa, Fla.: Brevard Community College, 1981. (ED 221 153)

Fersh, S., and Greene, W. (eds.). *The Community College and International Education: A Report of Progress.* Volume 2. Ft. Lauderdale, Fla.: Broward Community College, 1984. (ED 245 736)

Fifield, M., and Sakamoto, C. M. (eds.). *The Next Challenge: Balancing International Competition and Cooperation.* Washington, D.C.: American Association of Community and Junior Colleges, 1987.

Groennings, S. (ed.). *Economic Competitiveness and International Knowledge.* Regional Project on the Global Economy and Higher Education in New England. Boston: New England Board of Higher Education, 1987.

Hall, R. B. *Area Studies: With Special Reference to Their Implications for Research in the Social Sciences.* New York: Social Science Research Council, 1947.

Hess, G. "Internationalizing the Community College." In J. M. Perez Ponce (ed.), *Intercultural Education in the Two-Year College: A Handbook for Change.* Washington, D.C.: American Association of Community and Junior Colleges, Council for Intercultural Programs, 1976.

Icochea, L. "Bergen Community College." In E. L. Backman (ed.), *Approaches to International Education.* New York: Macmillan, 1984.

Jullien, M. A. *Esquisse et vues préliminaires d'un ouvrage sur l'éducation comparée. [Sketch and preliminary views of a work on comparative education].* Paris: 1817.

Mahoney, J. R., and Sakamoto, C. M. (eds.). *International Trade Education: Issues and Programs.* Washington, D.C.: American Association of Community and Junior Colleges, 1985. (ED 261 723)

Molkenboer, H. *Die Internationale Erziehungsarbeit, Einsetzung des Bleibenden Internationalen Erziehungrates. [International education work: Introduction of standard international quotas].* Flemsburg, West Germany: Westphalen, 1891.

National Governors' Association. *Making America Work: Productive People, Productive Policies.* Washington, D.C.: National Governors' Association, 1987.

Perkins, J. A., and others. *Strength Through Wisdom: A Critique of U.S. Capability. A Report to the President from the President's Commission on Foreign Language and International Studies.* Washington, D.C.: President's Commission on Foreign Language and International Studies, 1979. (ED 176 599)

Scanlon, D. *International Education: A Documentary History.* New York: Teachers College Press, Columbia University, 1960.

Shannon, W. G. *A Survey of International/Intercultural Education in Two-Year Colleges—1976.* LaPlata, Md.: Charles County Community College, 1978. (ED 164 034)

Southern Governors' Association. *Cornerstone of Competition: International Education. The Report of the Southern Governors' Association Advisory Council on International Education.* Washington, D.C.: Southern Governors' Association, 1986.

United States Congress. House. Committee on Education and Labor. Task Force on International Education. *International Education: Past, Present, Problems and Prospects. Selected Readings to Supplement H.R. 14643.* 89th Cong., 2d sess., 1966. H. Document 527. (ED 087 643)

David G. Scanlon is director of international education at Cape Cod Community College. He was professor of international education at Teachers College and has published numerous books on international education.

Strategies for implementing the goal of better world understanding are essential at the classroom level as well as throughout the institution.

Internationalizing the Community College: Strategies for the Classroom

Jane Edwards, Humphrey R. Tonkin

In the other chapters of this book, our colleagues document the now general agreement that we must bring our students to a better understanding of the world outside our borders; in this chapter, we will move directly to a practical consideration of strategies for those of us working toward this goal within the classroom.

We hold that internationalization of the curriculum is a matter that concerns all the academic disciplines and not just the liberal arts. Ideally, the effort to internationalize the community college will be sustained and college-wide, but even where faculty members work in a less-committed college, they can accomplish much within their own classrooms and in collaboration with sympathetic colleagues.

This chapter considers, in order of increasing ambition of effort, strategies for internationalization through working with international modules within courses, revision of course syllabi, the redefinition or revision of majors, and the use of reform of the general education curriculum as a means to institutionalize a significant international component across the campus.

The Individual Course

Internationalization begins at the level of the individual course. No field is so remote from the international sphere, no subject so local, that it cannot be viewed from an international perspective. Fields as unlikely as mathematics or nursing, chemistry or secretarial science have been successfully internationalized by individual faculty members over the past several years, and there are numerous examples of internationalized syllabi in virtually all fields available for our consideration (see Fersh and Fitchen, 1981; Fersh and Greene, 1984). Increasingly, publishers are producing textbooks with international elements incorporated into them, even on subjects that have hitherto been regarded as essentially local and domestic. Numerous organizations exist to help teachers at all levels increase the international component of their courses, and these organizations can help with syllabi, handbooks, and bibliographies (see Smith, 1988). International government organizations, such as the World Bank or the United Nations, publish materials either intended for educational purposes or readily adapted to them. These materials can frequently be used for comparative purposes. Thus, a course in labor relations in the United States can examine the labor situation in other countries, or a course in the United States Constitution can trace the influence of our constitution on constitutions in other countries and can explore the gap between constitutional expectations and constitutional realities in other societies as well as our own.

It is important also to remind our students that we live in a multilingual world. Even if they themselves lack the skills to handle materials in other languages, a faculty member may be able to cull examples or other materials from foreign-language sources to illustrate his or her own teaching. If students speak other languages at home, their services may even be enlisted to gather such materials, and the skilled faculty member may be able to incorporate these discoveries into the general life of the class.

Such internationalization of the individual course has the great advantage that it can be carried on by the individual faculty member working alone: There is no need to tangle with curriculum committees and academic hierarchies. It is important, of course, to check carefully on what is available before setting to work by making contact with national organizations, by checking on materials in the library, and perhaps also by considering how activities in a given course might be linked with ethnic groups in the community or with international firms in the vicinity, or with other local organizations. The assistance of foreign students, either at the college or at other institutions, might also be enlisted.

Working in the "Easy" Fields

Some disciplines are easier to internationalize than others. They are by definition international in orientation or are widely considered incomplete without an international component. We call these the "easy" disciplines because it is from these areas that an effort at internationalization across the campus can expand to include other disciplines. Few faculty members in a field such as anthropology, geography, foreign languages, art, or music will quarrel with the conclusion that their field is international by its very nature. These disciplines may thus be regarded as source disciplines, and it is frequently the faculty members from these areas who will be key participants in the international education effort.

Yet even in these disciplines, it is sometimes necessary for faculty members to revise their own perspectives quite radically. Thus the teaching of art and music may leave students with little idea that Renoir and Beethoven were not, under the skin, simply Americans. Paintings and musical compositions should be studied within their social and historical contexts. At the same time, these disciplines must move beyond considerations centered principally in Europe to provide students with insights into esthetic forms cultivated by other cultures and civilizations. As for American art or American music, and the phenomena of advertising and rock, which have swept large parts of the world, these can be explored in the economic and social context of a multi-cultural world. Foreign-language teachers often do not see the languages they teach as devices for opening a window on the larger world but merely as a means of learning about a second culture. Teachers of English sometimes forget that the English language has produced literatures of great worth and complexity in countries other than Britain and the United States. In the social sciences, faculty members can also reach beyond the world of English language publication, and fields such as anthropology and economics offer unlimited possibilities for internationalization at every level.

While much can be achieved by a teacher working alone, a cooperative effort within or between departments can bring greater success by encouraging others who might not take the initiative by themselves and by making possible an integrated approach to reform. Perhaps a group of colleagues from a single department will work together to effect changes in the department's offerings. Perhaps a cross-disciplinary group with a common interest in, say, public-policy issues or cross-cultural communication will decide to collaborate. Such a group might be well advised to seek the help of administrative units on the campus, particularly at a college that has its own international education office or offices for study abroad, or has foreign students.

There are numerous interesting examples of partial or complete reform of traditional departments in two-year colleges, but we offer an example from a four-year campus because it can so easily be adapted to the two-year setting. At the University of Maryland, Baltimore County (UMBC), a program entitled "The World of Language" teaches students the nature of language and offers a curriculum balanced between the studies of language, culture, and literature (Duverlie and Rosenthal, 1982). Students are guided toward the acquisition of practical language skills and cultural awareness, with literature as an added advantage rather than as the core of the program. A community college wishing to make foreign languages accessible to its students would do well to imitate the UMBC approach. An additional advantage with a program of this kind is that its broadened disciplinary base makes it accessible to other departments and helps give students the sense that their studies are integrated across disciplines.

While it is certainly possible for a political science department to offer a major based wholly on the government of the United States, or for a history department to teach only Western history and to leave students unaware of the great historical movements of the rest of the world, such cases are increasingly rare. Fields such as history and political science are almost automatically international in their perspective, and on a campus where internationalization is actively pursued, relatively small adjustments can usually ensure that these disciplines are internationalized. Other disciplines, such as sociology, are commonly more local and domestic in their focus. The American Sociological Association's compilation of syllabi and resources for internationalizing courses in sociology (Armer, 1983) is full of models to counteract this tendency. For example, one introductory course is built around a case study of the Bolivian highlands. This comparative approach to the discipline helps students gain objectivity, and no violence is done to the teaching of the analytical and methodological skills that must also be taught at this level. Similar possibilities are available to the faculty member in economics or in business studies.

Working in the "Less-Easy" Fields

Natural scientists face even greater problems than social scientists in emphasizing the international dimension of their field. Natural scientists frequently feel enormous time pressure in teaching complex analytical and methodological subject matter that they perceive as being objective in its very nature, and thus not merely international but universal. The actual community of scientists is perhaps more international than any community from the social sciences or humanities: Symbols travel more easily than words. It should be possible to put this fact to use by including international modules in science courses at all levels that investigate the question of how science is practiced, taught, or empirically relevant elsewhere in the world. Certainly the life sciences and geology provide a natural handle for grasping the importance of internationalization if faculty members choose to do so. Issues of ethics and of the environment are international by definition. And if faculty members are concerned about entering the territory of their colleagues in the social sciences, there are still some options available to them. They might invite these same colleagues into their classes to discuss such issues themselves, or, at the very least, they might draw their examples and problems from the international sphere. Even mathematics lends itself well to such an approach (Schwartz, 1979, 1980).

A fairly ambitious example of this approach to the natural sciences is provided by the module on "Photovoltaic energy conversion in developing countries," developed by Norman Abell of Brevard Community College (Fersh and Fitchen, 1981, pp. 201-210). This module addresses the uses of solar power in the developing countries and includes descriptions of research projects conducted outside the United States. Students correspond with international companies to obtain information about photovoltaic projects. Along the way, a good deal of information about conditions in several developing countries is incorporated. Above all, students gain a sense of industrial research as a phenomenon that is international by necessity in the interdependent world of the late twentieth century.

Just as the natural scientist must include a great deal of technical data in his or her courses, so faculty members in preprofessional programs are under pressure to include only material directly related to the professional training of their students. They must face and overcome the feeling that time spent on international matters is time taken away from something else. Even more than in the sciences, the modular approach is pragmatically the easiest to incorporate into the teaching of the technical disciplines. In many preprofessional fields—for example, in the health sciences—interpersonal skills will prove important to the student, and there may be good reasons for including in the curriculum preparation in cross-cultural communication and even preparation for work in an international movement.

In business administration the case is somewhat different, since international training is increasingly a necessity. The international business major at Middlesex Community College in New Jersey was an early example of the rethinking of an entire major, with specializations offered in several international fields and with outreach made to the local business community through a business round table (Council on Learning, 1981, pp. 60-61). Nolan McCuen, of Brevard Community College, has produced an innovative module for use in an introductory business administration course, involving study of United States business structures through a comparative approach (McCuen, 1981), which helps students develop a capacity for independent research and critical thought.

In the field of nursing there are also numerous examples of successful internationalized teaching modules. The module developed by Betty Chase (1981) explores the utility of exercise for health by analyzing Chinese attitudes to the question and by study of Tai Chi Chuan, traditional Chinese exercises.

The greatest difficulty in the way of internationalizing the "less-easy" fields has to do with the expectations and attitudes of faculty members. Thus the idea of using cooperative work between members of "easy" and "less-easy" disciplines and fields may be crucial to the success of efforts to internationalize the community college curriculum.

General Education

We often perceive internationalization as another component of the education of our students—like critical thinking or writing—that is primarily of concern to those educators who are attempting to give students a general level of culture and skills that will allow them to be successful in their chosen fields. On many of our campuses, however, the revision of general education is currently a priority, providing us with special opportunities to include an international component in the general curriculum. Hence the process of internationalization may well begin as a process of revitalization among faculty members responsible for the core programs of an institution.

At Broome Community College, New York, a six-year process has recently resulted in a complete revision of general-education requirements to include an international perspective that is being incorporated into the three disciplinary sectors English/Humanities, Social Science, and Science/Mathematics. A committee has defined the components of this perspective, including, among other things, a comparative perspective in all disciplines, knowledge of foreign languages and world geography, and some experience with global issues and with nonwestern materials (Romano, 1986). With Title VI funding, a program of workshops for key faculty members (and any others who care to attend) is under way. A side benefit of this integrated, multidisciplinary program is the development of a core of faculty members to share experience in the development of modules and the revision of syllabi. Ultimately, if a campus mandate exists, this experience may be used to assist faculty members in more technical fields to internationalize their own courses.

Ideally, a general education program will include interdisciplinary offerings of the kind that made up the general-education core at Los Medanos Community College, California, at its inception (Shannon, 1978, pp. 27–28). This program provided interdisciplinary packages covering behavioral, social, biological, and physical sciences, the language arts, and humanistic studies. Additional course offerings were planned to address broad topics such as "The Nature of Man in Society." Where good relations exist between faculty members contemplating change, it is possible to develop highly innovative programs of this kind. Where faculty members are more isolated, or where reform is less of a priority, other mechanisms need to be used to work an international perspective into the general-education programs—for example, the reform of individual courses.

For a faculty member teaching "Introduction to Cultural Anthropology" an international component is a given, but for the faculty member teaching freshman composition, an international component will be infused only by conscious effort. Here a different approach will be needed. The well-documented curriculum revision at Broward Community College (Fersh and Greene, 1984) involved, for example, the redefinition of introductory literature and writing courses to include nonwestern materials. Where major courses also fulfill general distribution requirements and are routinely open to nonmajors, as is usual in the liberal arts disciplines at community colleges, the internationalization of a major and of general education overlap: If in more advanced courses the international dimension of general education courses is reinforced, we can begin to achieve our goal of introducing a global perspective into the educational programs of the community college.

Faculty Development

In the process of internationalization, the problems faced by faculty members at community colleges are much the same as those faced by the faculty of four-year and graduate institutions, and the arguments for and against internationalization are much the same. The methods used to reform the curriculum are also similar. There is only one important difference: Faculty members at two-year colleges do not always work and operate in the cosmopolitan intellectual world common in our major universities. "Owing to the nature of community colleges, their curriculum and general goals," writes one educator (Hess, 1982, p. 122), "the faculty usually does not possess the kind of broad international academic background found at universities offering graduate programs and engaging in a variety of research projects." Hence, special support mechanisms will be needed and special incentives will need to be provided. The effort will probably begin with an inventory of the expertise available on the campus and identification of those faculty members who can provide a nucleus of commitment and experience. Faculty development will be essential.

Faculty development usually takes money. The institution must be prepared to assist financially. Many community colleges have been helped by grants available from a number of sources, particularly the Department of Education (Fersh and Greene, 1984, pp. 140-142). The ground-breaking program at Monroe Community College received funding from the National Endowment for the Humanities, the New York Council on the Humanities, and various local sources, in addition to major funding from the Department of Education.

In addition, if the administration of the college is sufficiently concerned, it can focus already available faculty development funds on internationalization efforts. If curriculum development in this area is seen as a priority, faculty members will soon come forward with ideas. Particular attention can be given to group projects. The model chosen by Broome Community College—a series of workshops presenting different ways of creating course modules, attended by core faculty members who are paid or otherwise rewarded for their attendance, and open also to others—is one effective way of proceeding. There are two things to bear in mind in this kind of activity.

First, all activities need follow-up. It is easy to attend a workshop, leave full of good intentions, and then allow oneself to be buried under the weight of other demands. Follow-up sessions, perhaps informal and less structured, are essential.

Second, workshop presenters must be carefully chosen and must make their presentations with a full understanding of what the needs and expectations of their audience may be. Poor workshops can derail entire programs. Sometimes people from outside the institution can offer a fresh perspective, but it is often better, and less costly, to use insiders who know the problems of the institution well and are available for consultation and follow-up activities.

Rewards for the completion of modules, revision of syllabi, and other curricular improvements are essential and should be made as public as possible. In addition, a balance has to be kept between the demands of internationalization and those of other curricular goals of the institution, and hence the involvement of a faculty committee to provide oversight and guidance is essential.

There are, of course, other means of faculty development than workshops on the creation of curricular materials or the revision of syllabi. Faculty members can be encouraged to seek outside funding to spend periods abroad, money can be provided by the institution for this purpose, and programs of paid leave can be modified accordingly. International exchange arrangements can be set up so that faculty members can have experience teaching in another country. Such initiatives are discussed elsewhere in this volume, but their impact on the curriculum itself should not be underestimated.

Conclusion: Working on the Curriculum

Infusion of an international perspective into the community college curriculum can be achieved through the use of modules, by the revision of syllabi, or by programmatic reform. New programs or courses can be established. Ideally, all of these methods will be used together to achieve the goal of an integrated curriculum. In addition, experiential learning, both within and outside the classroom, can help give meaning to classroom instruction. The process of internationalization may begin with disciplines avowedly international in nature and then turn to those fields where the international component is normally less pronounced. Examples of successful teaching tools are readily available, and these can be used as sources or models. There are also many available accounts of efforts to internationalize entire institutions, both community colleges and four-year campuses, and these may provide helpful guidance. But ultimately, each effort at internationalization will be different, and each college, after weighing its available human and financial resources, and after considering the overall mission of the institution, will choose its own way.

One goal, of course, must be authentic institutionalization, so that an international perspective becomes part of the fabric of the college, part of its tradition. Such institutionalization, if it is to be successful, must involve large numbers of people over a protracted period of time. These people must include administrators as well as faculty members, the campus officials concerned with admissions and student affairs, and of course those concerned with the raising of outside money. Priorities and programs in higher education come and go, but the development of an international perspective in our students is an imperative that must remain and be strengthened if we are to cope successfully with the century ahead.

References

Abell, N. "Photovoltaic Energy Conversion in Developing Countries." In S. Fersh and E. Fitchen (eds.), *The Community College and International Education: A Report of Progress*. Cocoa, Fla.: Brevard Community College, 1981.

American Assembly. *Running Out of Time*. New York: American Assembly, 1987.

Armer, J. M. *Syllabi and Resources for Internationalizing Courses in Sociology*. Washington, D.C.: American Sociological Association, 1983.

Chase, B. "An Instructional Module in Nursing: *Tai Chi Chuan*." In S. Fersh and E. Fitchen (eds.), *The Community College and International Education: A Report of Progress*. Cocoa, Fla.: Brevard Community College, 1981.

Cleveland, H. "The Revolution in Education for a Global Age." *Access*, 1988, 79, 1–8.

Council on Learning. *Education for a Global Century: Handbook of Exemplary Programs. Education and the World View, III*. New Rochelle, N.Y.: Change Magazine Press, 1981. (ED 210 238)

Duverlie, C., and Rosenthal, A. A. *The UMBC Language Program*. Catonsville, Md.: University of Maryland, 1982.

Fersh, S., and Fitchen, E. (eds.). *The Community College and International Education: A Report of Progress*. Cocoa, Fla.: Brevard Community College, 1981. (ED 211 153)

Fersh, S., and Greene, W. (eds.). *The Community College and International Education: A Report of Progress*. Vol. 2. Ft. Lauderdale, Fla.: Broward Community College, 1984. (ED 245 736)

Hess, G. *Freshmen and Sophomores Abroad: Community Colleges and Overseas Academic Programs*. New York: Teachers College Press, 1982. (ED 231 467)

McCuen, N. "A Self-Programmed Unit: Introductory Business." In S. Fersh and E. Fitchen (eds.), *The Community College and International Education: A Report of Progress*. Cocoa, Fla.: Brevard Community College, 1981. (ED 211 153)

Romano, R. "Internationalizing the Campus." *Common Knowledge*, 1986.

Schwartz, R. *Mathematics and Global Survival*. Staten Island, N.Y.: College of Staten Island, 1979. (ED 229 233)

Schwartz, R. *Mathematics and Global Perspectives: A Working Team*. New York: Global Perspectives in Education, 1980. (ED 233 876)

Shannon, W. G. *A Survey of International/Intercultural Education in Two-Year Colleges—1976*. La Plata, Md.: Charles County Community College, 1978.

Smith, A. F. "The State of Global Education." *Access*, 1988, 79, 9–13.

Tonkin, H., and Edwards, J. *The World in the Curriculum: Curricular Strategies for the 21st Century. Education and the World View, II.* New Rochelle, N.Y.: Change Magazine Press, 1981. (ED 211 009)

Jane Edwards is assistant professor at the University of Hartford, Connecticut. She was director of international education at the State University of New York at Potsdam and was with the Harvard Institute for International Development.

Humphrey R. Tonkin is president of the University of Hartford, Connecticut. He was president of the State University of New York at Potsdam and has been active in international education.

*An experienced director of international education gives some
practical advice for administrators of study-abroad programs aimed
at the general student body.*

The Effective Development of Nontraditional Study-Abroad Programs

William K. Spofford

The traditional study-abroad program is a junior-year abroad in a foreign university. In countries whose first language is other than English, such programs require a high degree of fluency in a foreign language. These traditional study-abroad experiences can be excellent, but they are accessible to only the handful of students who attain fluency prior to their junior year. The vast majority of students are excluded from programs of this type.

Fortunately, an equally legitimate, nontraditional model is available, one that addresses the pressing need for all students to have an international experience in order to be prepared for our increasingly interdependent world. Such a program is of a semester's or a year's duration; it is open to any qualified sophomore, junior, or senior, regardless of his or her major; and it is available in countries whose first language is other than English, regardless of a student's level of fluency in that language.

These two models imply very different responsibilities for the study-abroad director. In the traditional context, the director's role can be somewhat passive. Because prospective participants are fluent in a foreign language, they are already convinced of the importance of the overseas experience; they are primed to go and often take the initiative themselves. Therefore, very little selling needs to be done.

For the nontraditional program, however, the director must recruit much more actively because, first, the prospective participants—representing all majors—must be acquainted with opportunities they may simply never have known about, let alone considered; and, second, they must be persuaded of the value of participation. Therefore, a great deal of time and energy must be devoted to promotion and recruitment. Also, this model implies special considerations for the selection, orientation, and reentry of students. In this chapter, I will address in detail these key concerns, which are critical in the effective development of nontraditional study-abroad programs.

Promotion and Recruitment

Because all students are prospective participants in overseas educational programs, the first goal is to expose students to an in-person presentation. At the University of Wisconsin, Platteville, this cannot be accomplished in a single year short of an all-college convocation in the football stadium, which would be too big, too impersonal—and too cold in the winter. Therefore, in my work recruiting for the study-abroad program, I focus only on freshmen, who can be accessed through their required freshman composition sequence. By speaking to all composition sections in a given semester, virtually every first-year student can be reached, and after four years, I can be sure that every student on campus has heard the presentation.

In the beginning, I carried a slide projector and handouts from class to class. However, while speaking to small groups may have personalized the presentations, such a ride through thirty-five or more classes was a gruelling and time-consuming experience. In recent years, therefore, I have gained the same coverage in just two days in February by having the teachers bring their students to me at a central location. The English faculty are given the dates at their department meeting in November, so they can set aside a class period in their spring-semester syllabus.

In early February, students are beginning to be bored with their routines and depressed by the depths of the Wisconsin winter, and spring vacation is too far in the future to distract them with its visions of hot sands on Florida beaches. At the same time, however, they are certainly very receptive to fantasies of faraway places, especially if the temperature outside is ten below; slides of sunny Spain maximize the impact.

Not only is timing more convenient when classes are combined, but also the presentation is more effective when a central location is used. Both slides and videotapes can be integrated, refreshments can be served, and past participants can be utilized as resource people. Students usually will have questions of their fellow students who have already studied abroad, but even if they do not, it is still effective to have present past participants—real, live peers who have gone through the experience.

I begin the presentation by addressing three misconceptions that students have about study-abroad programs.

Misconception 1: You have to be fluent in a foreign language to study in a country where the first language is other than English.

This preconception is based on the traditional model of the junior-year abroad for foreign-language majors. However, all of our programs abroad offer course work in English for students who are not fluent in a foreign language; therefore, students will be able to study the language of the country they visit at their appropriate level—even at the beginning level—and take the rest of their courses in English. Needless to say, at the University of Wisconsin, Platteville (and at most other institutions in the United States), we would deny the overseas experience to 95 percent of our students if we required fluency prior to participation in the study-abroad program. On most campuses the only students who even approach fluency are the foreign language majors, but today students from all disciplines need the international experience. (Students who *are* fluent can, of course, take all their courses in the foreign language.)

Misconception 2: If you spend a semester overseas, you must stay in school an extra semester to make up for the credits missed.

All the courses we offer overseas are fully approved for credit and appear on our transcripts like any other courses. Many of our overseas courses count especially toward majors in the liberal arts and in business. Aside from this, all students, regardless of their majors, must fulfill our general university requirements, one component of which is an 18-credit package in the humanities and social sciences. Virtually every course we offer overseas can count toward these general requirements. Finally, every degree program has some room for electives, so students can still stay on track toward their degrees even if they have fulfilled their general requirements. The only time there is a real problem finding an overseas program for a student is if that student is a second-semester junior or first-semester senior and *must* have very specific courses in his major. In fact, another important reason for speaking to second-semester freshmen is to encourage them to plan ahead for their overseas experience so that it can be fully integrated into their overall academic program.

Misconception 3: A study-abroad program costs an arm and a leg.

Not necessarily. Obviously, some programs are *very* expensive, but others are not. For instance, the program we sponsor on behalf of the College Consortium for International Studies in Mexico (including airfare) costs the same as a semester on campus for a Wisconsin resident. When the overseas educational costs are greater than those for a semester on campus, the student's eligibility for financial aid may also be greater than usual; therefore, I encourage students not to reject the prospect of studying abroad out-of-hand for financial reasons but to talk with a financial-aid counselor. Interestingly, students who are paying nonresident tuition can study in our European programs for essentially the same cost, while students from private colleges in the consortium will actually pay *less* than their regular tuition.

I emphasize to students that additional costs, if any, for study abroad should be viewed as an investment in their education and in their future. Given the increasing interdependence of the global community, the educational benefits are fairly obvious. However, the personal benefits are not as apparent, so I do mention the increase in independence and self-sufficiency, in adaptability and flexibility, in achievement and goal orientation, and in the ability to communicate effectively and to work successfully with others, regardless of national, racial, or religious background, all of which the student is likely to gain from experience abroad. All these benefits will stand students in good stead regardless of the specific profession they pursue. Finally, the presence of an overseas experience on the students' résumés will help to distinguish them from other graduates seeking the same entry-level positions.

With these three misconceptions addressed, I move to the substance of the academic programs—the specific courses that are available overseas. Students today seem obsessed with taking courses that will train them for a specific entry-level position, so they are not very receptive to the idea of a semester abroad as an enriching experience. That is why I emphasize that our overseas courses can fulfill their degree requirements and why I stress the indirect, though very important, ways in which the experience contributes to the students' personal growth and thereby to their professional potential.

Because of students' "job training" mentality, it is natural for them to want to take specialized courses in their majors. However, since the students' major professors will probably prefer them to take the most specialized courses at home, students should try to take courses overseas that they cannot take on the home campus, preferably courses that capitalize on the unique location and on the special expertise of foreign faculty. For instance, it would seem more appropriate and more interesting while in England's cultural and political center to study courses like Theatre in London and British Government and Politics than to take Anatomy and Physiology or Differential Equations.

The curricula offered overseas consist essentially of courses about the country in which they are studied so that the classroom experience complements and enhances the rest of the experience. In our Spain program, for instance, a student will study the Spanish language at the appropriate level, plus History of Spain, Art of Spain, Government and Politics of Spain, Comparative Social Problems, Spain and the European Economic Community, and so forth. The more the students know about the country in which they are living and studying, the better their experience will be. The curriculum is structured on this basis.

More Promotion

In addition to attending presentations in their freshman year, each student is contacted three times—first, with a promotional piece in the registration packets of incoming freshman; second, with a direct mailing in the summer following the freshman year; and third, with essentially the same direct mailing in February of the sophomore year, when the impact of those materials is reinforced by other promotional activities, including advertisements and articles in the school newspaper, notices in daily announcement sheets and on the local television notice board, interviews on the campus radio and television stations, displays in the library and elsewhere on campus, and flyers posted throughout the campus. The impact of the two direct mailings is reinforced by sending a complementary letter to parents; by inserting references to study-abroad courses in the University catalog, in adviser's and advisee's handbooks, in lists of courses recommended for general-education requirements, and in checklists for majors and minors; by recommending study-abroad veterans to be peer advisers and resident assistants in the residence halls; and by encouraging study-abroad veterans to help promote the programs.

In summary, the goal is to make direct contact with every student four times at roughly six-month intervals (during summer registration, through freshman-class presentations in February, in the first direct mailing in July, and in the second direct mailing the following February), with a concentration of publicity annually in February to reinforce the presentations for freshmen and the direct mailing to sophomores.

I also look for small ways to reinforce awareness of the program between those key times. Right before pre-registration in November and in April, all faculty receive a note asking them to encourage their advisees to integrate a study-abroad semester into their academic plans.

Adopting a suggestion from Dr. Jack McLean, director of International Education at Mohegan Community College, I also ask the faculty advisers to provide names of students who would be particularly good candidates for study abroad. I then send letters to those students, telling them that Professor X has recommended them for a study-abroad program because they have the necessary academic talent and personal maturity to succeed in and benefit from the experience. Finally, in August I send a letter to all honor students (those with a 3.25 or better grade-point average), congratulating them on their eligibility for study-abroad scholarships.

For our local promotional mailings, the University provides mailing labels in zip-code order, and we enclose (1) a letter explaining the importance of the overseas experience, (2) flyers outlining the basics of our two major programs (London and Seville), and (3) a postpaid card (bearing the University's first-class permit number) on which students fill in their name and address and check off the programs about which they wish further information.

Such coverage can certainly stimulate interest on a campus, but further recruitment may be necessary if a minimum number of students is needed to guarantee a program. Such was our situation when we needed forty students to start our London program, and we could not rely on our own pool of students to meet the minimum each year. Instead, we secured student directories from other campuses in the Wisconsin state-university system, established parameters for each director based on information available in the directories (primarily the semester or year in school and major of each student), hired student workers to type mailing labels, and mailed information packets to students throughout the university system.

Selection

All students need a significant international component in their education simply to be prepared for the interdependent global community into which they will graduate and in which they must function both as citizens and as professionals. This need can be met somewhat through course work on the home campus, but the best preparation is through living and studying in another country—a total experience, both cognitive and affective. The period of study should be of several months duration simply because a two-week study tour—say to Rome, Florence, and Venice—is like going through another culture in a glass box. You look at the outside of the culture: In Eudora Welty's phrase, you drive past things that happen to people—you are in the culture, but not of it.

While all students (regardless of their major) are encouraged to consider an overseas program, all students who apply are not accepted. Our programs are open to all qualified sophomores, juniors, and seniors because junior year (the designated year in the traditional model) may not be the most appropriate time for all majors to participate. But we do not accept freshmen because we want them to have a full year to adjust to the American higher educational system—the logical and natural extension of their previous years of schooling—before taking on a different educational system in a different cultural setting. It is easy to forget that adjusting to college can be a challenge for some eighteen-year-olds, and they must have the opportunity to make that transition and get their feet firmly on the ground before being given significant variations in a foreign environment.

A 2.5 or better cumulative grade-point average (on a 4.0 scale) is generally required. This average may seem low in comparison with the traditional, exclusive programs, but it reflects our commitment to all students, not just to the French major with honors. Our philosophy is inclusive rather than exclusive because we believe that all students need the international experience simply to be prepared to live and work in our world. We feel that a 2.5 cumulative average indicates that the student has successfully made the transition to college-level work and has established himself or herself as a solid student; that is, one who stands a reasonably good chance of succeeding academically overseas despite the adjustments required and despite the marvelous distractions that students will—and should—take advantage of. Students with less than a 2.5 cumulative average who have very solid grades in the humanities and social sciences, but poor grades in mathematics and the natural sciences, are generally accepted since almost all overseas work is in the humanities and social sciences.

Orientation

The second year I led a two-week study tour in Italy, one of the recruits told me that she had dreamed of visiting Italy all her life. When I hear that kind of comment now, a red flag goes up, but I was too inexperienced at the time to spot the potential problem. During our two weeks in Italy, we saw the greatest art treasures of Rome, Florence, and Venice, yet throughout the two weeks, this student was dissatisfied. While other students were thrilled to visit the Sistine Chapel and to stand in the presence of Michelangelo's David, these experiences just did not live up to her expectations.

I learned from this student. Now I go out of my way to brainwash the students—that is, to inculcate a certain mind-set that minimizes preconceptions and expectations; that wipes the slate as clean as possible. "Hope for the best, but expect the worst," I tell them. "That way you'll never be disappointed." It is much better to have very modest expectations and be pleasantly surprised than to have inflated expectations and be disappointed—especially when the reality will be the same no matter what attitude a student approaches it with.

This mental preparation is a constant concern from the very first contact until the day of departure, and it plays a part in virtually every conversation that I have with students. In addition, such considerations are addressed in writing in our formal orientation materials. It is much better to present the program realistically and honestly—even if it discourages the romantics—than to glamorize it.

Along the same lines, if your students are involved in cooperative programs that you do not directly administer, as early as you can put them in direct contact with the program administrator at their affiliated American college. This will help to ensure that your students are getting the most up-to-date and accurate information, which is not guaranteed if all the information is filtered through you, as middleman, no matter how conscientious you are. Putting your students directly in touch with their school's administrator will enable the administrator to provide the most current information and will enable him or her to set the tone of the program and shape the attitudes of the students, which are ultimately more important than specific information itself.

However, students benefit greatly from orientation information that is specific to the program and from general information on intercultural issues. I provide students with memos offering practical advice; "Cultur-grams" from Brigham Young University, which provide a brief overview of a country's customs, manners, and lifestyles; and a contemporary history, taken mainly from *Time* magazine, of each country. Over the years, I have gathered articles on a variety of intercultural themes that I reproduce for the students. In addition, I provide them with two other publications from Brigham Young University, "Coming Home Again" and *Intercultural Interacting,* and the booklet *Survival Kit for Overseas Living* from Intercultural Press. Although providing these books to every student is a significant expense, it is well worth it.

Reentry

A former colleague of mine in international education used to tell me that his only job was to set up the program and that it was up to the student to have a good experience. While there is some truth in this idea, the director's responsibility continues through every stage of the program and does not end even when the grades are issued and all outstanding questions are resolved. There is more to be done. Every semester I have a meeting of all study-abroad veterans, particularly to welcome home the most recent return-ees. We view and discuss an excellent videotape called "Welcome Home, Stranger," we have some pizza, and we talk about our experiences overseas and our reentry to the United States. This meeting brings recent returnees immediately on their return to campus into contact with older veterans. It provides a peer group and a support group for them.

In addition, veterans are involved through their participation in our recruitment and orientation. This involvement is helpful to students considering a study-abroad program or getting ready to participate in one, and it is therapeutic for the veterans themselves because it provides a captive and very interested audience to whom they can talk about their experiences. Finally, I encourage veterans to join our International Students Club, which expands their conception of "peer group" and enlarges and enriches their support network.

Conclusion

I have no "helpful hints" regarding the everyday routine implicit in the nontraditional model of study-abroad programs presented here. I spend a lot of time talking with students and colleagues, in person and on the phone, on campus and off campus. Obviously, there are no hints there.

Much of what I do is to act as an intermediary between the students and the overseas institutions. My only suggestion on this point is to minimize turn-around time, which is just common sense. Finally, many of the problems with which I wrestle—curriculum, housing, transportation, financial aid, program payments—vary so much from program to program and circumstance to circumstance that few, if any, general rules can be formulated.

However, I have one very important tip for upper-level administrators: Give substance to your commitment to international education by appointing a full-time director. Do not assign an enthusiastic and energetic faculty member to the job on a part-time basis. A friend of mine once accepted a 40 percent assignment to start overseas programming from scratch, while trying to internationalize the campus and the curriculum, coordinate faculty exchanges, and advise foreign students. Two years ago he left education altogether.

The cause of international education is too important to the future of our students and our country to settle for lip-service and a part-time director. It demands resources as well as words. A full and genuine commitment is essential if we are to prepare our graduates for their place—both as citizens and as professionals—in the interdependent global community of today.

William K. Spofford is director of international education and professor of English at the University of Wisconsin, Platteville.

Administrative support as well as careful planning and thorough execution can result in a successful faculty exchange program that contributes to professional development and international awareness.

Facilitating Faculty Exchange

Brenda S. Robinson

Competence in international affairs has become a major educational concern. Reports abound in academia and industry of the woeful state of the knowledge of U.S. residents of cultures other than their own. Much-quoted Allan Bloom states that "Young Americans have less and less knowledge of and interest in foreign places. Practically all that young Americans have today is an unsubstantial awareness that there are many cultures . . ." (1987, pp. 34-35). Bloom's comments emanate from a discussion on "relevant" education in the United States.

The question of how to "make other cultures relevant" to U.S. students must extend beyond the question of maintaining economic primacy. Issues involving the United States, such as migration and changing demographics, the interdependence of nations, nuclear disarmament, concerns of peace, famine, and nutrition, and world-health crises require knowledge of, and ability to function within, other cultures in order to be effectively addressed. Bringing knowledge to the classroom is the province of educators—of teachers at every level—and they most likely have had limited (if any) experience of another culture.

One means of reducing intercultural illiteracy is through faculty exchange. The opportunity to live abroad, interacting within another culture at work and in community involvement, can help teachers bring the "relevance" of that culture to their classrooms on their return. Academic exchange—which has an extensive history from Fahien who traveled from China to India in 399 A.D. for scholarly pursuit (Keay and Mitra, 1978), and the revered academics who came to universities at Bologna (Ross, 1976) and Paris (Brickman, 1972), to the creation of the Rhodes and Fulbright scholarship programs—has documented many benefits. Continued support of this activity can assist in expanding the knowledge of our nation through direct classroom involvement.

This article is intended to be a "how-to" primer rather than a philosophical treatise on the value of exchange programs. Current trends indicate that institutions interested in such programs are well aware of the benefits gained. The most pressing need is how to establish them.

Prerequisites to Exchange

Colleges often enter into an exchange program through happenstance rather than through a conscientiously planned program. A foreign visitor offers to send a faculty member from his or her institution to the college; a professor travels abroad and receives an offer to teach at another institution for a specified period of time; a hopeful sabbatical applicant receives a Fulbright Teacher Exchange assignment. In most instances, the exchange— while an exciting prospect—is undertaken with little thought given to how it can enhance the professional development of the participants, how it meshes with an institution's mission, and how the details of the exchange will be handled. Planning, as with any project, is the key to the success, or downfall, of exchanges.

How does a planned exchange fit a given college's mission, goals, and objectives? Do international endeavors have the support of the institution's board of trustees and the full cooperation of the president? Is there sufficient commitment from the administration to choose participants carefully and to provide the necessary support for pre-departure planning and for hosting the incoming scholar? Are there sufficient resources, financial and human, to carry out the program? If a bargaining unit exists for faculty, does it recognize the exchange experience as relevant for promotion and tenure?

Many exchanges are begun without the slightest acknowledgment of the necessary philosophical and administrative bases required to ensure as successful a program as possible, and they succeed. However, the lessons learned from experience support the need for full consideration of the questions stated above prior to commitment to exchanges.

Each participating institution should assign exchange-program responsibilities to an administrator (or faculty member with release time), assuring that the person has sufficient time and personnel resources to carry out the program. An exchange program is labor-intensive at specific points in the program, requiring a person who can attend to detail, mobilize the college community, and facilitate program components outside the nine-to-five, Monday-through-Friday work week.

Program accountability includes many factors. The need for qualitative planning and administration is a given. Sufficient staffing and funding are essential. Maintaining direct contact with the exchange institution overseas should include a plan of yearly campus visits, perhaps establishing a calendar of alternating visits, to document program standards. Ideally, if institutions can establish a "twinning" or sister-school relationship and develop student, administrative, and support-staff exchanges as well, a comprehensive international program can be created.

Exchange Agreements

Two types of exchanges are prevalent, those that are sponsored programs (for example, the Fulbright Teacher Exchange) and those that are negotiated between institutions or groups of institutions. Sponsored programs have well-defined objectives, are generally funded by nonuniversity or noncollege sources, and provide external support systems for participants. The focus of this chapter will be negotiated programs.

All academic exchange programs should be documented in a written agreement that covers the following topics:

1. Goals and objectives
2. Terms of exchange (time parameters, number of exchanges per year, academic disciplines and teaching responsibilities, required supplemental responsibilities at the host institution, finances, health insurance, office space, supplemental funds, bargaining-unit issues, travel costs, accommodation/transportation exchanges, institutional responsibilities upon return, provisions for emergency return
3. Duration of the agreement.

It is suggested that the agreement permit each institution to be as flexible as possible, yet set specific responsibilities to facilitate the exchange. Agreements should be translated into the language of the overseas institution, if applicable, and copies in English and in the host institution's language should be signed by the chief executive officers of each institution.

Small colleges may wish to consider forming a consortium and writing an exchange agreement on behalf of the entire membership. This arrangement permits a sufficient pool of faculty from which to choose appropriate exchange participants and ensures that the exchange does not terminate for lack of faculty involvement.

Recruiting, Screening, and Selecting Participants

Recruiting faculty for an overseas exchange presents a challenge. Faculty concerns include time commitments, family commitments and priorities, considerations arising from dual-career marriages and ages of children, tenure and promotion considerations, and questions regarding finances and housing. A college must be convinced of the benefits of an exchange program and be willing to negotiate unique arrangements in order to facilitate participation. Exchanges on a semester basis are viable in some situations. Some colleges build the exchange into a sabbatical program, supplementing salaries with non-tax-levied funds. Exchanges with institutions in the Southern Hemisphere, where the academic calendar differs from the United States, also may be worked out.

Recruitment strategies include announcements in college publications and letters to each eligible employee. Following up this advertisement, it is important to attend departmental meetings to discuss exchange opportunities and to present program goals and faculty benefits. It takes time to accomplish this, of course, but the investment is beneficial.

Many an exchange program has encountered serious difficulties by choosing inappropriate participants. Academic criteria—discipline, scholarship, and professional reputation—are obvious selection criteria. Equally important are the personal characteristics of the applicants; a top scholar may not be the best choice. Qualities that enable exchange programs include flexibility, ability to adapt to new and stressful situations, cross-cultural understanding, problem-solving skills, and a sense of humor. Ideally, applicants who have traveled overseas have an advantage. It must be cautioned, however, that those who are used to traveling first-class often have great problems participating in exchange programs. These individuals are accustomed to having a U.S. living style replicated throughout the world and have not adapted to in-country living. They often see themselves as experienced world travelers and are the most affected by culture shock when placed in a position of fending for themselves in a foreign nation.

A written application form that meets the needs of the program and a current résumé should be the minimum for applicant selection. It is suggested that applicants also describe what they hope to contribute and gain from the experience.

Emphasis on selecting participants is essential. The make-or-break aspect of an exchange program lies in selection. A demanding, elite academician can do irreparable harm to your program, regardless of scholarship. The warm, friendly, humorous participant solicits next year's applicants.

Visas and Health Insurance

Incoming exchange faculty must have valid U.S. visas for the type of work they are to accomplish. This generally means a J-1 visa, issued through the host U.S. institution via an IAP-66. Obtaining State Department permission to issue IAP-66 documents requires formal application (and approval) from the U.S. State Department. The process must be initiated well in advance.

A J-1 visa permits an overseas faculty member to receive a U.S. salary and *may* exempt the participant from U.S. taxes. It also requires the faculty member to return to the home nation for two years following the exchange.

The IAP-66 documentation enables overseas faculty to obtain a visa easily and meets the U.S. government regulations pertaining to administration of exchange programs.

J-1 visas *require* participants to have health insurance valid in the United States from the moment they deplane through the time of departure. It may be possible to include the visiting scholar in the college's health plan. If not, a number of plans specifically designed to meet this type of program exist.

As with all visas, there are many stipulations accompanying a J-1. Administrators should be aware of all such parameters prior to formalizing an exchange program.

Faculty going abroad must also be concerned with obtaining the appropriate visa for the nation where they will teach. Tourist visas generally are not valid. As in the United States, entry visas must be obtained. Entry visas require valid documentation from the overseas college, in accordance with its nation's laws.

Additionally, the coverage provided by the U.S. participant's health-insurance policy should be investigated and correlated with requirements in the overseas country. Insurance agencies that provide health insurance to incoming scholars also provide coverage to faculty going overseas.

Pre-Departure Briefing

The more information participants have on the overseas nation, its higher educational system, the overseas college, and the resident community, the greater the chance there will be for successful adaptation by participants. There are many print materials available to assist administrators on this aspect. The consulate office of the overseas country will supply much information. Additional pamphlets and publications that are helpful include the following:

- CULTURGRAMS, available from Brigham Young University
- Nation-specific briefing materials from the U.S. State Department
- National Association of Foreign Student Affairs (NAFSA) publications
- Travel books.

A college may wish to prepare its own guidebook for participants in exchange programs. Also included should be the prospectus (catalogue) of the overseas institution, syllabi of course assignments, texts for the courses that will be taught, and information on how students are assessed and graded in the overseas college. Teaching methodology is crucial, as many nations employ the British or French system of instruction.

Faculty will be inquisitive about the conditions of daily life in the city or village where they will reside. Topics such as shopping, cooking, household help, utilities, public school systems and calendars, transportation, health and dental care, personal safety, religious services, and community activities are important. This information can often be obtained by the overseas college and forwarded to the U.S. participant.

Exchange professors should discuss the program and its parameters with previous participants, if possible; this permits them to compare personal experiences with the print information they receive. Additionally, putting the exchange professors in contact by telephone prior to their respective departures alleviates much anxiety. This is essential if they are exchanging housing as well as teaching posts.

A recommendation made by many experts is to assist the departing faculty member in acknowledging his or her own personal heritage and values as well as the cultural patterns of the United States. The more one knows about one's self and one's culture, the easier it is to adjust to another culture. It is those who are not aware of what they and their culture value who must then discover these in a foreign environment. The result can be devastating.

Communicating with Incoming Exchange Faculty

All of the necessary preparations for U.S. faculty going overseas must also be accomplished with the foreign faculty coming to the United States. This often necessitates many telephone calls detailing teaching responsibilities, housing arrangements, costs involved, and cultural and living-arrangement information. The more information is shared with all exchange participants, the fewer problems there will be after the program commences.

Return Briefing

Perhaps the most neglected aspect of exchange programs is the consideration of adjustment on the return home. Participants have had an incredible experience and are not the same people who, a year ago, left the college to go overseas. Those who remained at home remember the person who left and do not know the person who is returning. Preparing participants for the cultural shock on returning home and the reactions of colleagues to their experience is essential to quality programming.

Post-Exchange Activities

Publicizing the program enhances the institution's commitment to exchange programming and assists with recruitment of future participants. In-house, community, national, and overseas public relations should be included.

Prior to the departure of participants, the college should develop an action plan to utilize the participants' experience gained overseas when they return. Often, exchange programs do not recognize the skills and knowledge acquired by faculty overseas. The issue of acknowledging this experience in the promotion and tenure review process has been mentioned. In addition, the college now has a person with valuable skills to assist in curriculum development, promotion of international programs, public speaking, and public relations. The returning faculty member generally has a high degree of energy and creativity gained from the experience. To ignore the value of this experience—to ignore the returning participants—is all too common—and defeats the purpose of the program. The institution should capitalize on every aspect of the program through forms of public recognition and publication.

Hosting an Overseas Faculty Member

All the factors addressed in preparing a home faculty member for work overseas should be included in the preparation of foreign faculty coming to the United States. Collaboration with the overseas institution in designing the program components, including pre-departure briefings, is imperative. Visas; health insurance; living arrangements; teaching assignments, syllabi, texts, and course particulars; ancillary responsibilities; and finances are topics that should be addressed four to six months prior to the arrival of faculty.

The host college has obligations to the visiting faculty. Such immediate courtesies as meeting the faculty at the airport on arrival, providing assistance with orientation to the community, assisting with the establishment of bank accounts, providing telephone numbers for assistance and stocking the home refrigerator with sufficient food for the first few days are requisites.

If the college has an orientation program for new faculty, the visitor should be included. College regulations, policies, and procedures should be presented on arrival. A formal introduction to the college community and a welcoming reception should be planned. The program administrator should plan a hospitality program for the visitor, one that includes the visitor in the social and sight-seeing activities of the community. If possible, the host college should set aside a small amount of money to accomplish the hospitality program.

Local community programming is an additional consideration. The public school system and area service clubs are most interested in having overseas visitors speak. While caution should be exercised against over-programming, the inclusion of such community activities augments the program.

Conclusion

International programming can benefit greatly from commitment to faculty exchange. The ultimate recipients are not only the faculty involved but

44 Developing International Education Programs

their students—here and abroad—the college community, and the local community. With affirmation and support from an institution's administration, as well as thoughtful planning and considerate execution of the program, a successful exchange program for faculty can be a major contribution to the professional development of educators and to international awareness.

References

Backman, E. L. *Approaches to International Education.* New York: American Council on Education/Macmillan, 1984.

Baldassare, M., and Katz, C. *International Exchange Off-Campus: Foreign Students and Local Communities.* New York: International Institute of Education, 1986.

Bloom, A. *The Closing of the American Mind: How Higher Education Has Failed Democracy and Impoverished the Souls of Today's Students.* New York: Simon and Schuster, 1987.

Brickman, W. W. "Historical Perspectives on the International Component in Teacher Education." *Notre Dame Journal of Education,* 1972, 3 (3), 249.

Council on Learning. *Education for a Global Century: Handbook of Exemplary Programs.* New Rochelle, N.Y.: Change Magazine Press, 1981.

Goodwin, C. D., and Nacht, M. *Absence of Decision: Foreign Students in American Colleges and Universities, A Report on Policy Formation and the Lack Thereof.* New York: Institute of International Education, 1983.

Goodwin, C. D., and Nacht, M. *Decline and Renewal: Causes and Cures of Decay Among Foreign-Trained Intellectuals and Professionals in the Third World.* New York: Institute of International Education, 1986.

Keay, F. E., and Mitra, S. *A History of Education in India.* Calcutta: Oxford University Press, 1978.

Kepler, J. Z., Kepler, P., Gaither, O., and Gaither, M. *Americans Abroad: A Handbook for Living and Working Overseas.* New York: Praeger, 1983.

Lippitt, G. L., and Hoopes, D. S. (eds.). *Helping Across Cultures.* Washington, D.C., and London: International Consultants Foundation, 1978.

McKay, V. *Moving Abroad: A Guide to International Living.* Wilmington, Del.: VLM Enterprises, 1984.

National Association of Foreign Student Affairs. *Standards and Responsibilities in International Education Interchange.* Washington, D.C.: National Association of Foreign Student Affairs, 1981.

Ross, M. G. *The University: The Anatomy of Academe.* New York: McGraw-Hill, 1976.

Sakamoto, C. M., and Fifield, M. L. *The Next Challenge: Balancing International Competition and Cooperation.* Washington, D.C.: American Association of Community and Junior Colleges, 1987.

Stewart, E. C. *American Cultural Patterns: A Cross-Cultural Perspective.* Yarmouth, Me.: Intercultural Press, 1985.

Webster, S. *Teach Overseas: The Educator's World-Wide Handbook and Directory to International Teaching in Overseas Schools, Colleges, and Universities.* New York: Maple Tree, 1984.

Zikopoulos, M., and Barber, E. *The ITT International Fellowship Program: An Assessment After Ten Years.* New York: Institute of International Education, n.d.

Brenda S. Robinson is state university dean for international education at California State University. Formerly, she was director of the Center for International Service at CUNY/The College of Staten Island and was founder and executive director of the International/Intercultural Consortium/Community Colleges of Massachusetts.

*A college interested in offering study-abroad options can provide
many high-quality programs to its students through consortial
membership and a modest investment of resources.*

Consortial Approaches to International Education

John J. McLean

Why should American colleges be committing resources to overseas educational experiences for their students? After examining that issue we can
examine the question of consortial approaches to international education
in its proper context. This chapter deals with how one international-edu-
cation consortium actually works, considers the advantages and disadvan-
tages of consortia, and concludes with an analysis of what types of colleges
might profit the most from consortial membership. The model consortium
in this analysis is the College Consortium for International Studies, or
CCIS. Founded in 1975, this consortium offers imaginative and demanding
overseas-study opportunities to U.S. students in eighteen different foreign
countries.

We can safely include language training, acquiring a sense of historical
perspective, and developing an informed appreciation of diverse cultures
among the revered goals in the pantheon of American educational values.
Obviously there are other stated and unstated goals, but it seems safe to say
that the goals just enumerated are broadly, if not universally, accepted by
college faculties and administrations.

The argument here is that studies conducted in foreign locations
and cultures frequently meet the aforementioned goals and objectives
more completely than any educational experience we can devise on our
own campuses, and that these rich educational experiences are within
the reach of virtually all our students. Unfortunately, the evidence for
this assertion is largely testimonial and frequently anecdotal. Nonetheless, I believe that a common-sense case can be made that is persuasive,
if not conclusive.

NEW DIRECTIONS FOR COMMUNITY COLLEGES, no. 70, Summer 1990 © Jossey-Bass Inc., Publishers

The reemergence of historical studies, cross-cultural studies, and the new emphasis on foreign-language training coincides with the appearance of a new movement to internationalize the nation's curriculum. We are being forced by historical and economic events to readdress educational objectives and strategies in a new context. It remains to be seen, of course, whether program funding will follow the enthusiastic rhetoric about internationalizing our curricula. Consortial study-abroad programming offers many colleges a realistic way to bridge the gap between program support and program funding.

History, language study, and cross-cultural studies should be essential components in the curriculum of any well-educated person. The relationship between these assertions and this chapter is that overseas study is the most effective way of achieving many of these goals, and consortial approaches to overseas programming is the most efficient way to do it. Put another way, cultural immersion is the most effective way to teach the language, history, literature, and values of other societies, and consortial programming makes that possible even for our smallest and least affluent colleges.

Advantages and Disadvantages of the Consortial Approach

What advantages do consortia offer to prospective members? The advantages include program variety, organizational stability, efficiency, low costs, and quality overseas programming. Consortial programming is the most efficient and prudent choice smaller colleges can make for a variety of reasons. For example, the CCIS offers programs from China to Sweden, from Scotland to Israel, and from Ireland to Colombia. The start-up expense, the time, and the attention required to begin an overseas program are considerable. The time, expense, and attention required to maintain a quality program are even greater. Consortia offer partial ownership in their programs, not simply access to these programs. New members get the very tangible advantages of major revisions in their curricular offerings without the attendant burdens of program start-up costs and maintenance, while program sponsors get the advantage of access to an ever-growing pool of overseas-study students.

Many institutions encourage foreign travel and study of other cultures, but the study emphasis frequently is limited and, in some cases, so repetitious that the programs drift toward the extinction that is reserved for other good, but lame, ideas. In some cases, the demise of a good program may be directly linked to the requirement, relocation, or death of an individual who generated the institutional support for a particular program. Successful programs do not simply happen even when the circumstances favoring them are exceptionally advantageous. When the prospects for success are as daunting as they are numerous, some institutions will channel their efforts into areas that promise greater educational returns. Consortia provide the continuity that is necessary in overseas programming, and they reduce the risks that may intimidate individual colleges.

Cooperation in consortial arrangements is common enough when the model for such exchanges is department- or subject-centered and the focus is on the shared academic interests of colleagues who, more often than not, are from socially, as well as intellectually, kindred colleges. Common-action programs from colleges representing a broad variety of American colleges are rare, indeed, because they involve both a common goal and an uncommon perspective.

Institutional leaders usually encourage common-cause meetings and contracts, but common-action organizations are another matter. If common-action consortia promise to include administrators, faculties, or student constituents in ways that do not circumscribe the independence or compromise the good names of the member institutions, you may win the support of the administrations and faculties of those institutions.

The simple fact is that common-sense academic programming is difficult to design and more difficult to sustain. When the enthusiasm for the activity wanes, as it is likely to do, who will be left behind, in effect, to labor in a high sun for an uncertain yield? If the answer to that question is only the committed, the failure of many consortia becomes immediately apparent. The question is, therefore, is it possible to create mechanisms and organizational forms that can sustain worthy educational ideas after the enthusiasm of the founding members has faded? Can we devise ways of building enough educational capital for the consortial trust to perpetuate itself?

There are, of course, many reasons why colleges ought to cooperate in certain academic ventures. If cooperation is apt to produce results that may be unattainable without cooperation, a clear case can be made for common action, especially when the price of cooperation is negligible. But consortia must always meet the test of not infringing on an institution's sense of independence, which participating colleges properly protect and cherish. Consortia are, by definition, confederates of sovereign educational enterprises, and the key word is sovereign.

Consortial arrangements provide realistic remedies for institutions that are committed to the concept of international education but lack the staffs, the budgets, and the experience to organize and sustain overseas programs. Consortia may also provide excellent alternative programs to universities that already have extensive and successful study-abroad programs. Consortial approaches allow U.S. institutions a vehicle to pursue language training and a broad range of historical and cross-cultural studies efficiently and at very modest costs. They also provide benefits to students that their own colleges cannot duplicate. Studying abroad provides special illumination for American students because it may be the only time in a student's life that he or she experiences life as a minority population. Ensconced in digs in Shanghai, Seville, Toulon, or Edinburgh, a student soon discovers that the operative assumptions of a lifetime no longer apply or apply in ways that the student understands poorly and incompletely. The cocoon of the American college experience shields the student from the commonalities of his or her experience as a young person in contemporary American society. That is not true in Dublin, Lund, Bogotá, or Rome.

One of the great and comforting facts about a consortium like the CCIS is that it works. It may be a mild overstatement to say that a college newly belonging to CCIS can have a functioning overseas program in eighteen different locations overnight, but it is literally true that membership to CCIS brings with it both the opportunities and the necessary administrative support to allow a college to begin registering its own students in its own programs the day that the college becomes a member of the group. In this case membership means plugging into an existing set of circuits. Plugging in, of course, is an altogether different matter from building a system of circuits. A college may elect to build its own international circuits, if you will, but it is not obliged to, and it does not have the headache of maintaining the system it has chosen to use. Even if an institution already has a significant overseas program, plugging in to an existing network offers significant advantages.

How Consortial Membership Works—A Hypothetical Example from CCIS

A specific example from a hypothetical new member institution might help to clarify how consortial membership works. Blakefield College, the hypothetical member, has had an on-again, off-again interest in overseas programming. Professor Nystrom has taken Blakefield students and some community members to Nepal every other year for the last four years, and Dean Johnson appeared committed to the idea of offering Blakefield students some real program alternatives within the existing college curriculum. But Professor Nystrom did not return from Nepal after one stay, and Dean Johnson took a position at another college. The program to bring foreign students to the Blakefield campus, moreover, really never took root and the faculty-exchange program, which generated real interest, was limited to an exchange of economics professors that took place over eight years ago. Nonetheless, the transparent advantages of overseas study continued to produce a low-level glow at Blakefield, despite years of neglect.

Three factors combined to reignite interest in international programming at Blakefield, however. The first factor was the decision to hire Professor Nance Breakthrough. The second factor was the growing consensus within the institution that Blakefield students performed poorly on tests that measured cross-cultural awareness, historical literacy (especially in nonwestern history), and genuine foreign-language fluency. The third factor was the decision by the college administration to join a consortium and to give Professor Breakthrough some released time in an effort to correct some of these deficiencies. Thus Blakefield began a process that contained all of the essential components for success. Blakefield had administrative support (specifically, presidential support), a willingness to provide at least a minimal level of financial support, and a faculty consensus not only that the endeavor was consonant with the educational objectives enunciated by the college but that, additionally, the endeavor offered the promise of helping the institution meet its stated educational objectives. Each of these components is essential to a successful international studies program. Perhaps the two most important elements, however, are presidential support and the commitment of the Professor Breakthroughs of the world.

What does a consortium such as the CCIS bring to the success equation? To begin with, it brings the experience of organizing (in CCIS's case) eighteen successful overseas-study programs that, in our hypothetical example, are now, not only at the service of Blakefield, but are, by virtue of consortial membership, Blakefield programs. Blakefield can register its own students in its own programs in Ireland, Sweden, Colombia, or China, to use a few examples.

To be even more specific, perhaps we might track the enrollment of a hypothetical Blakefield student in one of Blakefield's new study-abroad programs. The student (let us call her Jean English) is excited to discover that Blakefield has overseas-study programs offering Blakefield credit. (It should be noted that Blakefield is enrolling its own student in its own program, and the student will be receiving a Blakefield transcript.) Ms. English has always hoped to study in Ireland, and she presses Professor Breakthrough about the details of Blakefield's program in Ireland.

After scanning the CCIS Ireland brochure, student and mentor become aware of the following basic facts: The program in Ireland is cosponsored by Mohegan Community College, Connecticut, and Keene State College in New Hampshire. The program sites are St. Patrick's College in Maynooth, Ireland, and the University of Limerick. But will courses transfer, Ms. English inquires? Professor Breakthrough, who has done her homework, says yes, because as a member institution Blakefield is awarding the credit for its programs in Ireland. How does the student apply? Professor Breakthrough produces a standard application that is part of the packet of materials sent to her by the CCIS central office.

The application, in addition to the standard fare that such applications solicit, requires that the student submit three letters of recommendation signed by her professors, and, additionally, a current transcript must be sent to Professor Breakthrough.

With that material in hand, the questions arise about what to do next. Professor Breakthrough, who has been provided with the names and phone numbers of all of the directors of international education at all the member institutions within the consortium, simply calls Dr. McLean, who is listed as program director. As to what Professor Breakthrough is to do next, Professor McLean explains that with a few exceptions, it is up to Professor Breakthrough to determine whether or not her student has met the minimum stated requirements for this particular program.

Ms. English completes her Fall semester registration forms at Blakefield, and a copy of her file is sent to Dr. McLean. All aspects of Ms. English's program of study in Ireland, following her acceptance, counseling, and registration at Blakefield, are now in the hands of the program sponsor. Blakefield is advised to collect its own registration fees, a deposit from the student for the Ireland program, and any additional administrative fee that they might charge for their overseas-study office. (Administrative fees vary, but $150 to $300 is the approximate range for CCIS member schools.) Each program has what is known as the TPC, or total program cost, which is the amount that a member institution sends to the sponsoring institution. Blakefield, therefore, is obliged to collect the Ireland TPC, and forward it to, in this case, Mohegan Community College.

Additionally, the program sponsor handles the administration of housing in Ireland. As can be seen, in a very real sense, Professor Breakthrough's job has been minimized by the operating procedures within the Consortium. As she became more aware of the details of the various programs she was administering, she would rely less and less on the program sponsors for information details. But there would always be aspects of program administration that were the responsibility of the sponsoring institutions. For most small institutions or institutions with lean budgets for overseas programming, Blakefield may provide an example of how a consortial approach to international programming works. Blakefield has been able to register its first student for its program in Ireland with a minimum of administrative experience and after a very modest investment on the part of the college. Beyond the expense of membership, itself nominal, Blakefield gave Professor Breakthrough released time from two classes to administer their new overseas-study program. What the college gained in return was immeasurably greater, however, because the definition of Blakefield was changed, and Blakefield's curriculum was expanded in ways that provided new opportunities for, potentially, every student the college served.

If a Blakefield student wanted to take courses in international business or in Italian art and civilization in Florence or Rome, that was now possible. The process, furthermore, would not have been any more complex than the process of placing Jean English, the first Blakefield student in Ireland, to study Anglo-Irish literature and the other suite of courses that comprised that program. The range of opportunities offered by CCIS is considerable:

from language study at Harbin University to Hebraic studies at Haifa University, to studies at the University of The Americas in Mexico and at the University of Lund in Sweden. Blakefield, moreover, is not responsible for the ongoing administrative problems associated with maintaining this rather far-flung network of study-abroad opportunities.

In the case of colleges that already have some foreign-study programs operating in the same nations as existing consortial programs, those colleges may elect to use CCIS programs selectively and simply maintain their own programs, which they may have nurtured over the years. Blakefield, for instance, would not have been obliged to give up its program in Spain, if it had such a program, because the consortium had a program in Seville.

Overcoming Prejudice and Inertia, and Other Obstacles to the Consortial Approach

The advantages of the consortial approach to international studies programming seem wondrous indeed. Why haven't more institutions taken advantage of this arrangement, which is both efficient and inexpensive? The answer is linked to issues of institutional independence, institutional indifference, and the institutional failures of consortia themselves. The simple truth is that consortia do not always work as smoothly as the imaginary Blakefield model suggested.

Many American colleges have a long and successful history of continuous involvement with overseas institutions because those colleges and universities have always understood that the experience of living and studying abroad is, quite simply, matchless. There are experiences that cannot be replicated or enhanced on the campuses of our most storied universities, regardless of their antiquity or endowment of the presence of the finest faculties and facilities. The great colleges know that and plan the education of their charges with that fact in mind. There is in this a certain suggestion that the concept of the "grand tour" has always endured in the grand old colleges. Did living in France really improve one's French? Did it really expose a curious mind to a distinctively European perspective? Did it genuinely broaden what may have been a somewhat parochial point of view? The answer to that is that it did all of those things and more.

Opportunities to travel and study abroad were limited, however, to the students at the elite institutions who were, not coincidentally, part of the American financial and social elite. Perhaps, the very concept of foreign study as the peculiar prerogative of the elite, which we associated with the "junior-year-abroad" experience, became ingrained in our minds. In the case of foreign study we may be dealing with an idea that is one of the last outposts of what many people consider an exclusive enclave of the well-heeled. That is more than just distressing if, as I believe, it is true. That perspective undermines our ability to address our educational objectives with either the wit or the imagination that the task requires.

Of course, learning German in a setting where German is the only means of communicating is enormously more effective than three sixty-minute classes over several semesters at a state college with even our most gifted instructors. A course in Italian civilization that utilizes the museums in the Vatican and in Florence is more apt to achieve its educational goals than a similar course offered in the extension division of the community colleges in Newark, Topeka, or Seattle. So why don't we provide our students with more of these incomparable opportunities? For some administrators and faculty the idea is, frankly, unthinkable. For others the answer is too transparently obvious for serious consideration. Overseas programs cost too much, and they are neither appropriate nor necessary for the institution's students.

But if you start with the concession that some study experiences abroad are obviously more likely to achieve the objectives of your institution than any programmed experienced that the college might ingeniously create, that concession creates something of a logical dilemma. How can superior educational experience be dismissed as inappropriate for a college's students? It can only be inappropriate if superior educational opportunities and solutions are inappropriate to the educational mission of the college in question.

We may be posing the challenge of study-abroad programming in ways that are unattractive or uninspiring to the administrative decision makers who have the responsibility to determine how an institution's budget will be spent. The argument we offer is that overseas programming should be an integral part of the college curriculum at all of our colleges because it meets specific educational objectives better than any other type of institutional programming. Furthermore, the position of this essay is that quality, low-cost overseas education is available through consortia like the CCIS.

As professionals with a serious commitment to the education of our students, how would we respond to the following proposal? The proposal is that the college spend one-tenth of 1 percent of its budget for a program that promises to excite students, to alter the rest of their lives, and to endure as the educational experience that has most profoundly changed them. Who among us would hesitate to endorse such a program? In fact, that is precisely what students returning from programs abroad continue to tell their overseas-study advisers, not only when they first return but years later.

But who uses these programs? It may be that in the start-up period, in particular, less than 1 percent of Blakefield's students actually participated in the overseas programming. If that was the case there would be some rough symmetry between expenditures and student participation that would justify the program cost. But much more would have occurred than simply having sent students abroad. The existence of these new and imaginative options within the college would become far more widely known than participation levels would indicate, and they would stand as indicators of what Blakefield was all about.

Despite their promise, consortial approaches to international education sometimes do fail, and consortia themselves contribute to these failures. One problem that novice members to a consortium face is overcoming the sense of being outsiders at someone else's party. Of course, the veteran members of the consortial group ought to be sensitive to such concerns of new members, but frequently they are not. Consortia are confederations, and, lacking any central administration to turn to, new members may be neglected through inadvertence.

Probably the largest group of its kind, the CCIS has no problem in recruiting new members, but the consortium still faces the problem of member colleges that are really only nominal members. Students from such colleges do not participate in the consortium's programs, faculty and administrators do not utilize the consortium's professional development seminars, and the college never participates in any of the administrative committees of the consortium. It is difficult to imagine what benefits accrue to such members other than the fact that they may be able to satisfy themselves that membership frees them from any additional commitment to internationalizing their curricula. There is the additional issue of apathy, of course. In that event consortial membership falls into a category akin to that of payments for professional journals no one has read since they were first requested by the professor who, long ago, ran away with one of his or her students.

Conclusion and Caveat

It is easy to oversell the benefits of consortial approaches to international education because the benefits are genuine and the idea makes such good sense. It may be fitting, therefore, to end this analysis by reemphasizing that for all of the advantages that consortial approaches offer, the success of any study-abroad program depends on a minimal level of institutional commitment, consistent support from the college president or whatever dean may be charged with program oversight, and unflagging energy and enthusiasm from the program director. Given those prerequisites, a consortium can be of enormous value to institutions that recognize the relationship between international programming and their institutional mission statements. Without those prerequisites and without that recognition, a college is not likely to succeed in its attempt to offer its students an expanded and enriched international curriculum: Consortial membership cannot fill the void created by that lack of commitment.

John J. McLean is director of international education and professor of history at Mohegan Community College, Connecticut.

Community colleges can assist in developing two-year programs abroad in order to facilitate foreign student entry into U.S. colleges and universities.

Developing American Two-Year College Programs Abroad

William E. Greene

More than ten years have passed since President Carter's Commission on Foreign Language and International Studies called on community colleges to "enlarge their international commitment and engage in the staff development necessary to strengthen their contributions to foreign language and international studies" (1979, p. 116). The commission urged that a "special effort should be mounted in community colleges. They enroll close to half of all undergraduates but only a small fraction take courses in foreign languages or international studies" (p. 75).

Community colleges in the United States have become increasingly active in developing and offering international education programs. Expanded international components in the curriculum, international-business programs, faculty and student exchanges, staff-development projects, new methodologies in teaching foreign languages, and increased international student enrollments are evidence of a significant and growing commitment on the part of community colleges to international education.

As community colleges have become more sophisticated in their approach to international education, a growing number of institutions have participated in cooperative and technical assistance projects abroad. Some community colleges have established individual international linkages, while others have become involved through membership in consortia such as the Community Colleges for International Development, Inc. (CCID) or the International/Intercultural Consortium of the American Association of Community and Junior Colleges (I/IC of AACJC).

At the same time as community colleges have enhanced their international education efforts, increasing numbers of foreign students have chosen to study in the United States. The Institute of International Education (Zikopoulos, 1987, pp. vi–vii) reports that more than 340,000 foreign students were enrolled in colleges and universities in the United States during 1986–87. Slightly more than half of these students were enrolled in undergraduate programs, and approximately two-thirds were funded through personal or family sources. Taiwan, Malaysia, China, and Korea were the four leading countries of origin of foreign students in the U.S. during 1986–87, while European countries accounted for only about 10 percent of enrollments. The three most popular fields of study were engineering, business and management, and mathematics and computer sciences.

While the attraction to U.S. colleges and universities continues, some educational planners and government officials abroad have expressed concerns about the growing number of students seeking higher education in the United States. The financial cost of attending a U.S. institution for four or more years is substantial, both for individuals and families and for government sponsors. In strictly economic terms, U.S. education is an import for a student's country of origin, and large numbers of citizens studying abroad adversely affect a nation's balance of payments. Others are concerned about the possible effects of four years of living and studying in the United States on the social, political, and cultural attitudes of college-age students. For these reasons and others, programs have been encouraged in several countries that enable students to complete some of their U.S. degree requirements at home, thereby reducing the time spent in the United States. Several U.S. community colleges have assumed an important role in this process.

American Two-Year College Programs Abroad: The Example of Broward Community College

As American community and junior colleges have pioneered the university-parallel, two-year transfer model, it is logical that two-year institutions in the United States would become active in establishing American two-year college programs in foreign locations. When properly developed and structured, such programs can enable foreign students to complete one to two years of college-level work in their home country or region before transferring to colleges and universities in the United States. The advantages of this approach are many and obvious, and increasing numbers of foreign students will likely avail themselves of such opportunities in the future.

American two-year programs abroad are structured in several different ways. Some have loose or informal associations with U.S. colleges and universities, while others have established more formal linkages or affiliations. Most U.S. community colleges collaborating with institutions overseas provide curriculum assistance and guidelines for academic standards. Several two-year programs abroad utilize the course numbers, course titles, and catalogue descriptions of their U.S. partners. Occasionally, a two-year American college overseas, such as Franklin College in Switzerland, enjoys full U.S. accreditation; however, most do not. Overseas programs linked with U.S. colleges usually make reference to their affiliation in catalogues and brochures and on their transcripts. In some cases, the U.S. cooperating college actually issues an official transcript for students enrolled in the American program abroad. In almost every case, the full expenses of operating the program abroad, as well as the cost of affiliation with the U.S. college, is borne entirely by the overseas partner.

Broward Community College (BCC) in Fort Lauderdale, Florida, has developed a comprehensive international education program and has been active in establishing linkages with community-college programs overseas. BCC first offered study-abroad programs in 1974 and established a college-wide international education office in 1977. BCC is one of only a few community colleges in the United States to have an international general-education degree requirement. Students earning an Associate in Arts degree at BCC must earn a minimum of six credits in courses designated as having a major international or intercultural content and emphasis (Greene, 1984).

Broward Community College's first foreign academic affiliation program was established in 1981 with Columbus International College (CIC), located in Seville, Spain. This affiliation was a natural extension of a cooperative arrangement established in 1979 whereby CIC served as the Seville Center for the BCC/CCIS (College Consortium for International Studies) Semester-in-Spain Program. Since BCC/CCIS students were studying for a term or two at CIC and considerable communication occurred between the two institutions on a regular basis, it became advantageous for CIC to adopt the BCC curriculum. Faculty exchanges and increased curriculum assistance provided by BCC resulted. Library expansion also occurred as BCC donated several thousand books to CIC. Transfer to colleges and universities for regular students enrolled at CIC was facilitated due to the affiliation.

The affiliation between BCC and CIC was restructured in 1985 when CIC relocated to Marbella, Spain. From 1985 to 1988, CIC offered primarily Associate in Science degree programs in business administration and related areas, and BCC again provided assistance in developing and offering these programs. During 1988, CIC was restructured as the Marbella College of Higher Education and developed plans to offer four-year programs in cooperation with colleges in the United States and England. The BCC affiliation continued for Marbella's freshman-sophomore–level courses and programs. Additionally, BCC and CIC developed plans to establish an American college program in Buenos Aires, the first classes of which were offered in the fall of 1988.

The Center for International Studies (CIS) in Madrid is another example of an American college program in Spain. Founded in 1981 primarily as a study center for American students, the CIS gradually began to attract significant numbers of Spanish students and foreign residents interested in beginning their university studies in Madrid before transferring to colleges and universities in the United States. A broad selection of freshman-sophomore-level general-education courses are offered, with most courses taught in English. A most interesting feature of the CIS program is that Los Angeles City College and the University of Wisconsin, Stevens Point, issue official transcripts for students of the CIS program. Transcripts from accredited institutions in the United States obviously facilitate successful transfer by foreign students to American higher education institutions.

Brookdale Community College (Lincroft, New Jersey) has established an American community college program in Guayaquil, Ecuador. Developed in 1985 in cooperation with the American School of Guayaquil, the program enables local residents to earn up to forty-five college credits before transferring to Brookdale in New Jersey or to other U.S. colleges and universities. Students registered in the program receive a Brookdale Community College transcript (E. Baran, personal communication, March 17, 1988).

In 1983 representatives of Broward Community College were invited to visit with officials of Kolej Damansara Utama (KDU) in Kuala Lumpur to discuss the establishment of an American community college program in Malaysia. Increasing numbers of Malaysian students were studying in the United States, and the cost of obtaining a U.S. university degree was, and is, a considerable burden for privately funded students. The government of Malaysia was promoting a policy of privatization in many sectors of the economy, and this opened the door for the establishment of private, postsecondary institutions. It became apparent that a high-quality two-year American college program in Malaysia would attract large numbers of students.

BCC and KDU established an "Agreement of Cooperation" that remained in effect for nearly four years, from 1983 through 1986. During that time, KDU was academically affiliated with BCC and offered a two-year American-college curriculum leading to the Associate in Arts Diploma. KDU adopted the BCC curriculum, including course numbers and titles, catalogue descriptions, and course outlines. BCC academic standards, admission policies, general-education and degree requirements, and academic standards were utilized (sometimes with slight modification). KDU issued official transcripts for students enrolled in the American program. The transcripts included a reference to the affiliation with BCC and indicated that course descriptions were available from either KDU in Malaysia or BCC in Florida.

While KDU also offered several technical and vocational programs, the American program attracted large numbers of Malaysian students to the college. As enrollments grew, so too did the number of transfers to U.S.

colleges and universities. KDU and BCC were committed to establishing high academic standards, and KDU students performed well after admission to U.S. institutions.

Performance after transfer is, of course, the ultimate test. If students transferring from an American college program abroad succeed academically after admission to U.S. universities, critics will tend to judge the affiliation program a success. A study of Malaysian students attending colleges and universities in the United States (Silney, 1986) showed that students who had attended KDU demonstrated a high degree of academic success after transfer. KDU students now gain admission to and are even recruited by many competitive U.S. colleges and universities.

During the nearly four-year period of the affiliation, more than twenty BCC faculty members and administrators traveled to Malaysia and worked with their counterparts at KDU. BCC officials not previously involved in international education activities—such as the registrar, the director of libraries, and the director of learning resources—participated in the project. Several BCC faculty members taught during summer terms at KDU. All direct costs for the affiliation were borne by KDU. While BCC representatives gave freely of their expertise and talent, they benefited enormously from working in an international environment, through interaction with colleagues abroad, and in their association with the many dedicated professionals at KDU.

Other Examples: Malaysia, Singapore, Japan

Lincoln Land Community College (Springfield, Illinois) provided assistance for the development of another American community college program in Malaysia in 1983. Maktab Sains MARA / MARA Community College, located in Kuantan, Malaysia, was established by the MARA Education Foundation to provide educational services and training for *bumiputra* (indigenous Malays). MARA offered a two-year, university-parallel, American-style program patterned after the curriculum of Lincoln Land Community College, as well as an intensive English program and a pre-American-degree preparatory program. Hundreds of MARA students have transferred successfully to baccalaureate degree programs in the United States (Maktab Sains MARA, 1988).

As more and more Malaysian students seek higher education opportunities in the United States, Malaysian sponsors such as the MARA Foundation have sought to provide increased support and, at the same time, to control expenses. One way to accomplish this is, of course, by reducing the number of years Malaysian students are required to spend in the United States to earn a four-year degree. Partly because of the success of American two-year college programs, the Institute Teknolgi MARA (ITM) has encouraged the establishment of two-year undergraduate U.S. university programs in Malaysia. These programs, which are offered in cooperation with several U.S. universities and university consortia, offer course work taught by U.S. faculty, and provide transcripts from accredited U.S. schools. Accordingly, the credits earned are easily transferred to the United States (Stedman, 1986, p. 121). More than 3,500 students and 300 U.S. faculty were participating in the ITM program in Kuala Lumpur by 1987 (Reichard). The Institute of International Education reports (Zikopoulos, 1987, p. 18) that during 1986–87, more than 23,000 Malaysian students were enrolled in American colleges and universities, ranking Malaysia as the second leading country of origin for foreign students in the United States.

In 1986, Broward Community College and the ISS International School, Singapore, entered into a multi-year "Agreement of Cooperation" to develop the American College Program in Singapore. ISS was founded in 1981 in cooperation with International Schools Services of Princeton, New Jersey. ISS is registered with the Ministry of Education of Singapore, and the elementary and secondary school is accredited by the Western Association of Schools and Colleges. The American College Program was approved by the Ministry of Education in April 1986 and thus became the first American college program to be offered in Singapore.

Students enrolled in the American College Program at ISS typically complete from forty-five to sixty semester credits at the freshman-sophomore level before applying for admission on a transfer basis to colleges and universities in the United States. ISS has adopted the BCC curriculum and utilizes BCC's course numbers and titles, catalogue descriptions, course outlines, faculty criteria, and academic standards. Courses are conducted in English. BCC teams make approximately two on-site visits to Singapore each year to ensure parallelism and quality. ISS (not BCC) issues transcripts reflecting academic work completed. During 1987–1988, a BCC faculty member served as acting dean of ISS's American College Program.

Two U.S. community colleges are involved in programs in Japan. Los Angeles City College is collaborating with the Tokyo-American Community College in offering freshman-sophomore–level general-education courses for Japanese students wishing to begin their U.S. university studies in Japan. Courses are taught in English by American faculty. Los Angeles City College supervises the curriculum and issues the transcripts (D. L. Culton, personal communication, September 19, 1989). Edmonds Community College (Lynnwood, Washington) has completed plans for a branch campus in Kobe, Japan. Scheduled to open in 1990 with an initial enrollment of 300 to 500 students, the campus will offer academic transfer programs, occupational programs, and intensive English programs. The project is the result of a cooperative agreement between Edmonds and private business groups in Japan (Morgridge, 1989).

The Future

The continued growth and development of American two-year college programs abroad will require much cooperation and commitment. Certainly, the several areas described below are basic to future success.

• *Quality.* American two-year college programs abroad must be of sound academic quality. Everything possible should be done to ensure that faculty qualifications, admissions requirements, and academic standards meet United States standards. Sponsoring U.S. community colleges must encourage their overseas counterparts to commit the financial resources necessary to maintain academic quality, especially in the early years when enrollments tend to be small. Library holdings, learning-resource materials, and computer hardware and software require substantial capital outlay.

• *Parallelism.* Community college programs abroad that are academically affiliated with U.S. community colleges require regular and ongoing articulation to ensure parallelism. Courses and programs overseas that are represented as equivalent to those offered in the United States must be equivalent. The U.S. community college is, in effect, the guarantor of the quality and parallelism of the overseas program. Professional visits, faculty and administrator exchanges, and the sharing of curriculum materials must occur often and on a systematic basis.

• *Program Evaluation.* Periodic evaluation of overseas programs is essential. Reichard (1987) and others (DeLoughry, 1989) have recommended that American college and university programs abroad be reviewed regularly by U.S. accrediting commissions. Follow-up studies should be conducted to determine the academic success of students who have transferred to U.S. colleges and universities. Evaluation visits, consisting of representatives of the U.S. affiliate as well as outside evaluators, should occur on a regular basis.

• *Cooperation.* There has been a hesitancy among officials at some U.S. universities to recognize the validity of overseas community college programs. To be sure, cooperating U.S. community colleges have a responsibility to communicate with U.S. universities and to provide full and accurate information regarding programs abroad. Misrepresentations and misunderstandings must be avoided. Presentations at professional conferences such as those of the National Association for Student Affairs and the American Association of Collegiate Registrars and Admissions Officers should be arranged to share information about overseas programs and to respond to questions and concerns. While it is true that foreign students from American two-year college programs abroad will spend less time at the U.S. colleges and universities to which they transfer, it is also true that a door will be opened for many who might never have been able to study in the United States. When a program is newly established, universities may choose to accept transfer students on a provisional basis subject to one or two terms of satisfactory academic work in the United States. After several successful transfers, however, universities should accept qualified students as regular transfer students and even consider entering into an articulation agreement with the overseas community college.

Conclusion

The future of American two-year college programs abroad will be shaped by many factors. Basic to any expansion is the continuing attraction of the U.S. system of higher education worldwide and the concomitant receptiveness of U.S. colleges and universities to growing foreign-student enrollments. Some educators in the United States believe foreign-student programs should be limited or, at least, increased in price to pay the full cost of the education provided. Others (Goodwin and Nacht, 1983, p. 14) observe that higher education is one of the few export industries left to the United States that commands international respect and shows significant growth potential. Successful American two-year college programs abroad can significantly increase access for foreign students to the U.S. system of higher education. The United States will face increased competition from the British, the Australians, and others, and must continually adapt to a changing marketplace. Permitting students to complete up to half of their degree program in their home country is one way to respond and, at the same time, provide a significant service for many students who might otherwise be unable to avail themselves of U.S. educational opportunities. U.S. community colleges are pioneering this effort.

References

DeLoughry, T. J. "As the Race to Internationalize U.S. Colleges Heats Up, Concern Rises over Programs' Quality and Standards." *Chronicle of Higher Education,* June 21, 1989, pp. A21–22.

Goodwin, C., and Nacht, M. *Absence of Decision: Foreign Students in American Colleges and Universities.* New York: Institute of International Education, 1983.

Greene, W. "Area 8: The International/Intercultural General Education Requirement." *Community and Junior College Journal,* 1984, 55 (4), 18–23.

Maktab Sains MARA/MARA Community College. *Catalog: 1986/88.* Kuantan, Malaysia: Maktab Sains MARA, 1986.

Morgridge, B. "Edmonds Community College: Breaking More Ground." *Community, Technical, and Junior College Journal,* 1989, 60 (1), 64.

President's Commission on Foreign Language and International Studies. *Strength Through Wisdom: A Critique of U.S. Capability.* Washington, D.C.: U.S. Government Printing Office, 1979.

Reichard, J. "Pacific Rim Trip Sheds Light on Exchanges." *NAFSA Newsletter,* October 1987, pp. 1, 9–13.

Silney, J. In W. Smart (chair), *Educational Developments in Malaysia.* Panel conducted at the 38th Annual Conference of the National Association for Foreign Student Affairs, San Antonio, Texas, April 1986.

Stedman, J. B. *Malaysia: A Study of the Educational System of Malaysia and a Guide to the Academic Placement of Students in Educational Institutions of the United States.* World Education Series. Washington, D.C.: American Association of Collegiate Registrars and Admissions Officers, 1986.

Zikopoulos, M. (ed.). *Open Doors: 1986–87: Report on International Educational Exchange.* New York: Institute of International Education, 1987.

William E. Greene is director of international education at Broward Community College, Fort Lauderdale, Florida, and is a member of the Executive Committee of the College Consortium for International Studies.

Community colleges must find ways to make international education a meaningful reality that pervades all aspects of instruction.

Adding an International Dimension to the Community College: Examples and Implications

Seymour H. Fersh

International education in the U.S. community college has come a long way. When the community college system was created after World War II, it was designed, in the words of President Truman's Commission on Higher Education, "to serve chiefly local community education needs" (Vaughan, 1983). By 1978, times had changed, and the U.S. Commissioner of Education called on our colleges to "lead the way in rebuilding our commitment to international education . . . our community colleges can and must take the initiative on this crucial agenda" (Boyer, 1979, p. 14).

A year later, President Carter's Commission on Foreign Languages and International Education singled out the community college to have a "central role in the Commission's charge to recommend ways in which to extend the knowledge of our citizens to the broadest population base possible" (President's Commission, 1979, p. 16). In 1988, the American Association of Community and Junior Colleges (AACJC) affirmed that international education is now a proper and appropriate concern for community colleges. The *AACJC Public Policy Agenda* "Mission Statement" includes, for the first time, the commitment to help member colleges "more effectively meet the economic and cultural needs of the nation in an increasingly international environment" and help "focus on the emerging concept of 'global citizenship'" (AACJC, 1988).

Those endorsements and that encouragement did not come easily. As recently as the early 1980s, the president of a large, metropolitan, seaport-area community college in Florida was admonished editorially by the local newspaper for his leadership in international education. But despite this kind of negative response and the widespread criticism of the presence of international education in the community college, some leaders of our institutions (including the AACJC) emerged in the mid-1970s and began to introduce international education into their own colleges and to create consortia to explore evolving possibilities in such education.

We need to understand that this strong, widespread shift in our colleges toward a commitment to international education was motivated mainly by changes in the world, especially changes that directly affected community colleges. For example, foreign-student enrollments in community colleges increased substantially and proportionally during the past decade: Currently, the number is about 50,000, which is about one-third of the foreign students enrolled at the undergraduate level in the United States. Increasing numbers of immigrants, foreign tourists, and multinational corporations have made many American communities more international in nature. Moreover and overall, the U.S. economy has become increasingly internationalized.

Also during the past ten years, increased interest from abroad in the American community college has hastened the international involvement of our institutions. A growing number of foreign educators and government officials have visited our colleges and initiated contacts in order to initiate exchange programs. These visitors, many of whom were delegated to make changes in their country's educational systems, were especially interested in the community colleges and the new kinds of nontraditional technological and vocational instruction in which community colleges excel.

Organizing for International Education

The question now is not whether a community college should be concerned with international education; the questions are to what extent, in what ways, and for what purposes. International education in the community college is no longer optional; it must become an integral part of what we are and are becoming (King and Fersh, 1983).

How, then, to start? Or to continue? Often it is useful to start with a definition. At Brevard Community College, we define international education in its broadest sense as referring generally to all programs, projects, studies, and activities that help an individual learn and care more about the world beyond his or her community and to transcend his or her culturally conditioned, ethnocentric perspectives, perceptions, and behavior. International education should not only increase one's knowledge; it should also enhance one's wisdom and affinity with humanity.

The implementation of such a definition is best achieved, we believe, by considering international education more as a transcultural and transnational dimension, represented by a continuum on which specialized study also exists. For example, particular focus is given to specific aspects of the international dimension: foreign languages, general education, international studies, and internationalizing the business curriculum. Overall, however, there is the cohesive and continuing intent to internationalize the college and the community.

Implementing the International Dimension

There are now many community colleges that provide examples of how to implement international programs. In a general sense, all such programs could be placed on a pedagogical continuum from those that tend to be content- and course-centered to those that tend to favor an infusion approach with special attention to faculty development. In the following pages, I provide examples of various programs. This sampling is only representative, not definitive; the number and quality of programs are, fortunately, more than can be reported on here.

Brevard Community College (Cocoa, Florida). The implementation of international education at Brevard has moved rapidly because the administration and faculty have the support of the Board of Trustees for such programs and because the local community (Brevard County being the home of the Kennedy Space Center) is greatly affected by international tourism and commerce.

Brevard has implemented international education throughout the college through (1) a structured process for the involvement of the community and the college; (2) study-abroad programs; (3) internationalizing the curriculum; (4) proper and effective programming of international students on campus; (5) programs of an international and intercultural nature for the community; (6) student-, faculty-, and staff-exchange programs; (7) consultant and support services with foreign institutions; and (8) staff- and program-development activities (King and Fersh, 1982).

Each year Brevard enrolls about 200 of its own students in summer study-abroad programs, enrolls annually on its own campus an equal number of foreign students from about 50 countries, and has provided about 150 professional, international short-term assignments for almost 100 of its faculty. A central objective of Brevard has been to strengthen the international component of its general-education curriculum. In Brevard's approach, the cooperation of faculty is crucial because the college has not chosen to achieve its purposes by requiring specific content-centered courses. Rather, the college affects the curriculum (especially in the non-social studies courses) by increasing the number of faculty members who have benefited from meaningful transcultural study and experiences. Brevard does not require that faculty leaders of students' study programs abroad be experts in the areas to be visited; it does require that they be well aware of and implement the educational purposes of such programs, which include affective as well as cognitive learning.

Broward Community College (Fort Lauderdale, Florida). Broward Community College has a diversified international education program administered through its office of international studies. A central aspect of Broward's implementation is the requirement that each student matriculating for an Associate in Arts degree take at least six semester hours of international-intercultural studies within his or her general education requirement of 37 semester hours. The international-intercultural area "is structured in the form of an overlay requirement. Students are not required to take additional courses; instead, enrollments are redirected to already existing area requirements." The "key features" of this requirement are described in an article, "Area Eight: The International/Intercultural General Education Requirement" (Greene, 1984a, p. 18–23).

Greene provides additional examples of Broward's implementation of international education. Also, a description of several of Broward's international programs will be found in Chapter Six of this volume.

Lansing Community College (Lansing, Michigan). Lansing Community College's approach to international education is a good example of an emphasis on the growing economic importance of such instruction. The college believes that every student who graduates and enters business should be prepared to communicate with, work, and live in a multi-cultural, international environment.

To achieve these purposes, for over twenty-five years Lansing has been involved in activities that include affiliations with colleges abroad, faculty and staff exchanges, the development of textbooks and resource materials, information exchange, professional-development programs, consultant services, and a student academic work-study program abroad. Members of the Lansing Board of Trustees have also traveled to and met with faculty, staff, and students in sister colleges in Korea, Japan, and the Republic of China (Taiwan).

Lansing has internationalized its curriculum, and has recruited and hired faculty and staff members who are U.S. citizens born and educated in other countries. Many of these faculty also have had business or industrial experience. Thus, many LCC faculty and staff members are bilingual and are familiar with the history, culture, and society of their homeland.

Valencia Community College (Orlando, Florida). From Valencia Community College there is available a very useful, concise outline of "How to Institutionalize International Education at Your College" (Ribley, 1987). Under "Creation of a Program," for example, several actions are recommended: centralizing international education activities, establishing a college-wide standing committee on international education, developing a long-range plan for international education for the college, and obtaining approval of the college's Board of Trustees for a policy statement on international education for the institution. The college also conducts faculty seminars in global cultural awareness and utilizes faculty consultants from university area-study centers.

Middlesex County College (Edison, New Jersey). Middlesex County College's international education program moved ahead in two major ways: through faculty involvement in changing existing courses and through special attention to college services to the business community. A report coauthored in 1980 by the college's president and its director of international studies noted that "it is as important to study and understand other people as it is to know ourselves and our own country" (Channing and Blanco, 1981, p. 6). This objective was achieved when the college, initiating its planning for international education in the late 1970s, first invited interested faculty to work as a curriculum team. Five faculty members were selected from among fifty-eight college-wide applicants, each representing one of the undergraduate divisions of the college: business, health technologies, science, engineering, and liberal arts. This group also served as a steering committee.

To serve the business community, the college surveyed its specific training needs in international trade and then provided a variety of services including convening a series of conferences and round-table meetings for the business community with representatives of organizations such as the World Trade Council, the World Trade Association, the New Jersey Business and Industry Association, and the American Society of Travel Agents.

Bergen Community College (Bergen, New Jersey). Bergen Community College is a leader in its objective to develop and infuse into its curriculum international and intercultural concepts based on the theme of global interdependence. Under successive grants from the federal government, Bergen has produced dozens of cross-cultural teaching modules, designed for six to twelve hours of instructional time. Some titles of the modules illustrate their variety: "Themes in Cross Cultural Music Appreciation," "Biological Methods of Childbirth and Delivery in Other Cultures," "Cross-Cultural Perspectives of Concepts in Physical Education," "African Perspectives of Mental Health," "Cross-Cultural Themes in Early Childhood Education," and "Introduction to Computers: A Cross Cultural Comparison of Educational Methodology" (Icochea, 1984).

Bergen also provides leadership for the business community in its metropolitan area. Its International Trade Round Table, for example, includes over seventy companies, which send representatives to monthly seminars and workshops. Bergen offers an A.A. degree in International Marketing and certificate programs in many areas of international trade. It also has a parallel degree and certificate program in International Studies.

Los Angeles Community College District (Los Angeles, California).
For examples of outstanding leadership in study-abroad programs, consider
requesting materials from the Los Angeles Community College District (Culton, 1983). One of their publications describes the purposes and history of
such programs in the district, outlines information about supervision and
administration, and has very useful "addenda" that include the kinds of
references especially helpful when one is starting such programs. The
District has also provided leadership for the California Consortium for
International Education.

Sources and Resources in Community Colleges

A community college's decision to initiate and implement an international
program should involve its trustees, administration, and faculty. When all
agree to implement such a program, one of the best actions to perform
next is to designate someone as director or coordinator of an office of
international programs or services who will then be able to provide leadership and services for colleagues and the college. This director should be
able to attend conferences on international education in the community
college in order to learn about what other colleges are doing and to develop
contacts with practitioners and providers. He or she should also become
knowledgeable about existing international education consortia and make
recommendations for appropriate members for his or her college.

The director can also learn about sources and resources that can be
helpful in specific ways; for example, basic references such as "The Directory of Resources for International Cultural and Educational Exchanges"
(U.S. Information Agency) and the "International Funding Guide" (American
Association of State Colleges and Universities). Also a regular reading of
AACJC's Community, Technical and Junior College Journal and the newsletter
of the AACJC International/Intercultural Consortium will provide a steady
source of news items, articles, and references related to community college
involvement in international education. In addition, many individual
community colleges and consortia issue helpful newsletters; see, for example, *Perspectives,* which is published seasonally by Cuyahoga Community
College.

Specific Implications for General Education

When initiating, organizing, and implementing an international dimension
in a community college, those responsible for leadership should give conscientious attention to the central importance of general education. While
it is true that the United States' need to be politically and economically
competent and competitive internationally is advanced by the study of
international subjects and foreign languages, we as educators must also

help our students achieve the personal benefits that can come from trans-cultural education and experiences. These kinds of opportunities should be an integral part of a general-education curriculum that affects all students regardless of their academic and occupational goals.

The subject of general education is the student. A crucial pedagogical concern of the international component of general education is to help the student become aware of the ways in which cultural conditioning leads to ethnocentrism. In its largest sense, international education involves learning not only about others but also about ourselves: how and why we are alike and how and why we are different, how we became the way we are, and what we can become (Fersh, 1989).

We humans surpass all other living species in our ability to learn from our ancestors and from each other. We also are the only species capable of making self-fulfilling prophecies; consequently, what we believe about ourselves is crucial. Unlike heavenly bodies, which go their own ways regardless of our theories about them, we are highly influenced by theories about ourselves.

Until recently, what we believed was largely a matter of personal choice. "Know thyself" has been urged on us for over two thousand years, mainly on a take-it-or-leave-it basis. Presumably, individuals who lived "reflective lives" personally gained thereby; those who did not were the losers, but their loss did not threaten others. Times have changed. In this century, human observations of the Earth from the moon have helped confirm visually what technology and ecology have been demonstrating—that we now live in the equivalent of an interdependent global village.

Challenged and confronted now by the certainty that people increasingly will live in cultures that are less and less extensions of their pasts, we now have the opportunity and the need to be culture-creators as well as culture-inheritors. Transcultural studies can help us transcend our cultural conditioning by enabling us to encounter culturally different minds. In the process, each mind is reminded that its viewpoints are mainly cultural rather than natural. Besides gaining knowledge of others, we also gain insights into what has become our "second nature." In a sense, cultural studies can be a kind of cultural psychoanalysis, where unconscious group mores and folkways are made conscious. We will need this heightened awareness because, increasingly, we will need to become more self-directing—that is, to become our own teachers and to continue a lifelong process of self-education.

While as teachers we do not have the right to insist on the specific values that students should hold, we do have a responsibility—some would say an obligation—to help students learn what values are, how we gain and modify values and what the connections are between what we profess to value and how we behave. The progress of humanity can move in opposite—but not necessarily opposing—directions: toward a culture of greater individualized choice and toward a global society in which all of us serve, share, and benefit.

In Chinese, the word "crisis" is written by combining the symbols for "danger" and "opportunity." The major motivation for increasing our international and cultural studies may have come from a sense of danger, but the crisis—properly conceived—is also full of opportunity. How each community college implements its international dimension will depend on its own purposes, procedures, and personnel. The community college system is so diversified that it is not possible (or desirable) to prescribe uniform techniques for achieving educational objectives. Much more important is an awareness of goals. How far and in what ways we continue are questions that will be better answered because of what we learn from those opportunities for personal development that help us transcend our cultural limitations.

References

American Association of Community and Junior Colleges. *1988 AACJC Public Policy Agenda.* Washington, D.C.: American Association of Community and Junior Colleges, 1988.

American Association of State Colleges and Universities. "International Funding Guide: Resources and Funds for International Activities at Colleges and Universities." Washington, D.C.: American Association of State Colleges and Universities, 1985.

Boyer, E. L. "Keynote Speech at the Annual AACJC Convention." *Community and Junior College Journal,* 1979, 49 (6), 14-19.

Channing, R. M., and Blanco, V. "A Transitional Outlook." *Community and Junior College Journal,* 1980, 51 (4), 6-10.

Culton, D. L. *International Education Programs.* Los Angeles, Calif.: Los Angeles Community College District, 1983.

Fersh, S. *Learning About Peoples and Cultures and Guide for Teachers.* Evanston, Ill.: McDougal, Littell and Company, 1989.

Fersh, S., and Fitchen, E. (eds.). *The Community College and International Education: A Report of Progress.* Cocoa, Fla.: Brevard Community College, 1981. (ED 211 153)

Greene, W. "Area 8: The International/Intercultural General Education Requirement." *Community and Junior College Journal,* 1984a, 55 (4), 18-23.

Greene, W. "Broward Community College: International/Intercultural Program." *Community and Junior College Journal,* 1984b, 55 (4), 18-23.

"Internationalizing the Curriculum at Lansing Community College." Paper presented at the International/Intercultural Consortia of the American Association of Junior and Community Colleges International Conference, Dallas, Texas, April 21, 1987.

Icochea, L. "Global Dimensions in an International Curriculum." Cited in S. Fersh and W. Greene. *The Community College and International Education: A Report of Progress.* Vol. 2. Ft. Lauderdale, Fla.: Broward Community College, 1984.

King, M. C., and Fersh, S. "General Education Through International/Intercultural Dimensions." *New Directions for Community Colleges,* 1982, 10 (4), 49-57.

King, M. C., and Fersh, S. "International Education and the U.S. Community College: From Optional to Integral." *ERIC Junior College Resource Review.* Los Angeles: ERIC Clearinghouse for Junior Colleges, 1983.

King, M. C., and Fersh, S. "Implementing the International Dimension: A Welcome

Imperative." *Community College Humanities Review,* 1987, 8. (ED 233 780)
President's Commission on Foreign Language and International Studies. *Strength Through Wisdom: A Critique of U.S. Capability.* Washington, D.C.: U.S. Government Printing Office, 1979.
Ribley, J. "How to Institutionalize International Education at Your College." Paper prepared at Valencia Community College, Department of International Studies, Orlando, Fla., 1987.
U.S. Information Agency. "Directory of Resources for International Cultural and Educational Exchanges." Washington, D.C.: U.S. Information Agency, 1987.
Vaughan, G. B. "President Truman Endorsed Community College Manifesto." *Community and Junior College Journal,* 1983, 53 (7).

Seymour H. Fersh is professor of humanities at Brevard Community College, Cocoa, Florida. From 1978 to 1980, he was director of international services for the American Association of Community and Junior Colleges.

Technical-assistance programs overseas promote world understanding and professional development at home.

Foreign Technical-Assistance Programs

Maxwell C. King

Foreign technical-assistance programs involving community colleges are a relatively recent development. There were few such programs before the late 1970s. It was the general perception widespread among community college leaders and trustees that community colleges had been created to serve local needs—mainly and usually needs that existed within the college's geographical area.

This perception of the community college's main function is still held by many people, including some administrators and teachers. Changes in this perception are occurring, however, because the nature of our communities is being affected by developments in areas outside those communities and especially by developments in the global economy. Many local communities are attracting foreign companies, and many local businesses are increasing their sales abroad. Florida alone exports annually $5 billion of goods and services—about the same dollar amount exported by entire nations such as Colombia, the Philippines, Greece, and New Zealand; in fact, Florida's annual dollar value of foreign trade is more than that, individually, of eighty-two countries (Moran, 1988).

Developments in the world have affected community colleges in other ways. Until a decade ago, our colleges were neither well known nor much respected abroad. These perceptions, too, have changed. Now delegations of foreign government officials and educators come frequently to our colleges to learn more about our programs—especially about how we train and educate workers for technology-related occupations. These visitors are also interested in how we involve community resources in cooperative educational efforts.

Meetings with foreign educators initiate exploratory talks concerning ways in which mutual benefits can be derived from foreign technical-assistance programs. For our colleges, we see the value of faculty development programs in helping the United States to compete in the world economy. The involvement of community colleges in foreign technical-assistance programs is now increasingly perceived as an integral part of what we need to do for our own good as well as that of others in order to provide the kinds of education and experiences that all of us will increasingly need.

The Community Colleges for International Development (CCID)

The CCID is a consortium of forty-four U.S. and Canadian community colleges. When it was founded in 1976 it had six members. An article written in 1979 identified the principal mission of the consortium as providing mid-level manpower training and technical assistance in occupational, vocational, and technical education to developing nations (Breuder and King, 1979). Today, the three central objectives of CCID still begin with providing assistance to other countries in mid-level manpower training and technical and vocational education; the other two objectives are to provide opportunities for international study, exchange, and professional development to students and faculty of U.S. community colleges and cooperating institutions abroad and to provide leadership and services in the development of programs in international education in community colleges.

To achieve these objectives, the consortium purposely started with a small institutional membership whose leaders were compatible and committed. Also, their institutions were diverse in geographical location and educational specialties. Colleges in the consortium are willing and able to provide educational and technical assistance through many kinds of arrangements. Interested countries may send students and faculty to member colleges, where modern and well-equipped instructional facilities plus well-prepared faculty are available, or they may request on-site technical assistance, or they may do both. Long-term (generally six months or longer) and short-term training programs are available. All technical assistance and educational programs are jointly designed and implemented by the international partners.

The story of how CCID began to implement and achieve its objectives is best understood by relating case-study examples of its first bilateral technical-assistance agreements, made in 1980 with the Republic of Surinam and the Republic of China (Taiwan).

CCID and Bilateral Agreement

The initial contact with the Republic of China was in 1978 when nine administrators of CCID colleges visited Taiwan at the invitation and expense of the Republic's Ministry of Education. The purpose of the trip was to establish inter-institutional linkages between CCID and junior colleges and technical institutions in Taiwan (Harper, 1980).

The initial contact with Surinam began with a conference in 1979 at Brevard Community College and was funded with assistance from the Organization of American States (OAS), the Tinker Foundation, and local Brevard County organizations. The conference title was "Mid-Level Manpower Training in Postsecondary Education"; it was attended by representatives from twenty-one OAS-member countries, senior officials from selected educational and funding organizations including the OAS, and the presidents and project officers of CCID colleges.

Subsequent bilateral agreements usually began in ways similar to the circumstances just described; that is, the agreements were usually preceded by either a visit of a CCID delegation to a host country or by making contacts at a consortium-sponsored conference. To understand the process in some detail, let us consider how the bilateral agreements with Surinam and the Republic of China proceeded.

CCID and Surinam

The bilateral agreement with Surinam evolved from the 1979 conference, which was attended by Roy Adama, inspector general of Surinam's institutions of vocational and technical education. He was seeking contacts and financing in the United States and from the Organization of American States to help his country develop its mid-level technical and vocational training and education. Mr. Adama was especially interested in working with U.S. community colleges because he believed that our services were most appropriate for his country. Surinam, formerly Dutch Guiana, became independent in 1975 from the Netherlands. Surinam's national language and medium of instruction is still Dutch, but English is widely understood and used.

In December 1979, the executive director of CCID accepted an invitation to consult in Surinam. Five months later a bilateral agreement was signed between CCID and the Ministry of Education and Community Development of the Republic of Surinam. Under this agreement, programs were designed providing assistance for vocational and technical training that included programs for students, teachers, and administrators.

One program in teacher training had individual Surinamese students attend a CCID college for a two-year technical or vocational degree, followed by a year of teacher training for the entire group of students at one specially designated member college. Another program is the enrollment of students with industry-acquired vocational skills as teacher-interns at a CCID college. Also, school administrators from Surinam have participated in management institutes conducted by the consortium.

A significant event in the consortium's relationship with Surinam was a conference convened in Paramaribo in April 1982 under the joint sponsorship of Surinam, the OAS, and CCID. This conference was a follow-up to the one in 1979. The major objective of the conference, focusing on the Caribbean area, was to encourage, facilitate, and implement transnational and regional cooperation in educational projects. Participating in the conference were representatives from the ministries of education of six Caribbean countries, officials from the OAS, six presidents and staff members of member colleges, and twenty-five educators from Surinam who were designated as official observers. The official record of the conference is available in a twenty-four-page report from CCID (Fersh and Humphrys, 1982).

CCID and the Republic of China

The first official contact with the Republic of China in 1978 was followed by a bilateral agreement between CCID and the Republic, signed in 1980. The original agreement continued in effect until it was superseded, in 1986, by a new agreement that runs for a ten-year period.

The initial projects under the first agreement focused on exchanges at the highest administrative levels. In the ten-year period from 1979 to 1989, about 125 American community college leaders visited Taiwan for ten-day study tours. These leaders were almost exclusively community college presidents and board trustees. Also included were leaders of the American Association of Community and Junior Colleges (AACJC) and project officers from member colleges in CCID. In exchange, from the Republic of China came an annual delegation of Chinese educators who visited colleges within the consortium. They also scheduled their visit so that they could attend the annual conference of the AACJC.

Exchanges at the instructional level also are implemented. From the Republic of China has come an annual corps of about forty teachers who have served one-semester internships at selected consortial colleges, usually from two to four interns at a particular host college. The Chinese visiting teachers are welcomed and accepted as colleagues, both for their professional expertise and as representatives of Chinese culture, thereby enhancing the transcultural dimension of the college and community. A summary report for a recent five-year period indicates that a minimum of ninety-one different academic areas were presented by visiting faculty, that forty-six colleges in Taiwan sent participants to the United States, and that forty U.S. community colleges served as host institutions.

Faculty from member colleges have provided instruction during summers in Taiwan. One major area of teaching has been English as a Second Language (ESL). These courses have taken different forms. For example, one was designed as an Intensive English Practicum. Four American instructors provided a one-month's program for forty-five junior college and technical school teachers from institutions throughout Taiwan. The Chinese participants included many of those who would later serve internships in the United States. In another year, the ESL program was designed for teachers of English in vocational and technical colleges in Taiwan. About one hundred of them participated in a program that was designed and taught by five visiting American teachers.

Other summer courses in Taiwan provided by CCID college faculty are technical workshops. In one year, for example, workshops were conducted on "Industrial Automation," "Tool and Die Making," "Competency-Based Curriculum," and "Industrial Safety." The American participants consisted of four visiting professors; forty-seven Chinese from diverse technical and vocational institutions took part in the workshops. Similar types of workshops have been offered in Taiwan each summer since the Republic of China–CCID agreement began. Each time, the instructional programs include attention to methods of teaching as well as subject matter.

CCID and Other Bilateral Agreements

Once CCID was under way, momentum grew in many ways, both from inside the organization where we were becoming more experienced in our international work and from outside the consortium where demand and opportunities for foreign technical-assistance programs were increasing. In the past six years, the consortium has signed bilateral agreements with the Technical University of Budapest, and Czech Technical University in Prague, the Association of Colombian Universities, the Supreme Council of Egyptian Universities, and the Maharashtra Federation of College Principals' Association in India.

All of these agreements were negotiated following a pattern the CCID initiated with the Republic of China; that is, the agreement was preceded by a visit to the foreign host by a delegation of presidents from member colleges. In the specific instance of India, the arrangements were somewhat different. Three CCID presidents and a staff person were invited to India for three weeks by the U.S. Educational Foundation in India, which administers the Fulbright program. The group presented a series of seminars on "Vocationalizing the Curriculum." During a session in Bombay, contact was made with the Secretary General of the Maharashtra Federation, which resulted in the bilateral agreement. The Federation includes about 600 colleges.

Separate Projects by CCID Members

Other kinds of foreign technical-assistance programs have been initiated and implemented by individual CCID members that have developed their own competencies and connections. These programs are too numerous and diverse to identify and describe here, but references to them appear in the CCID newsletter, *International News*. In the winter issue of 1988, for example, there is reported a wide range of international education programs conducted at over twenty CCID colleges. A report from Essex Community College (part of the Baltimore County Community College district) notes that twenty-three community-health workers from Belize participated in a training program under the auspices of the Central American Peace Scholarship Program. The one-month training program was designed to improve workers' clinical skills and to promote health at the village level.

The item above illustrates a foreign technical-assistance program in which many community colleges are involved. For example, the Central American Scholarship Program (CASP) and the Central American Peace Scholarships (CAPS) are special projects, financed by the U.S. Agency for International Development, designed to provide qualified, economically disadvantaged Central American students the opportunity to study in the United States on fully funded scholarships.

The programs, established in 1985, are administered by Georgetown University through partnerships with U.S. community colleges, and, to date, over 400 scholarships have been awarded. CASP/CAPS projects may be either for two years (for students wishing to receive an Associate Degree) or for three to six months to upgrade technical skills. The programs also include ESL instruction and extensive orientation to American life.

Thus far, our examples of foreign technical-assistance programs have been taken from the experiences of CCID and its member colleges. There are, however, many examples of community colleges and consortia that are actively and effectively involved in bilateral and other kinds of international arrangements.

Working with Companies and International Organizations

Community colleges can also participate in foreign technical-assistance programs by becoming subcontractors rather than signatories to bilateral or other agreements. For example, Brevard has benefited from working with private companies that enter into contracts to provide technical assistance abroad. Such a company is Educational Innovation Systems International (also named EDUSYSTEMS), which describes itself as a major supplier to vocational education projects, representing over 300 manufacturers of vocational and technical equipment. EDUSYSTEMS also provides services for all phases of vocational training projects, for which they recruit educators, for short-term and long-term assignments, from community colleges.

Another example of such organizations that subcontract with community colleges is the Training Division of General Electric Corporation. Our college contracted to train teachers from Turkey, who enrolled in Brevard's air conditioning and heating study program. They were participants in a G.E.-directed technician training project, which included about seventy trainees from Turkey, who received training at other community colleges in the United States and at technical institutes in the United Kingdom. The overall G.E. project was financed by the World Bank. G.E. has many similar projects for which it subcontracts.

The World Bank is integrally involved in foreign technical-assistance programs. It is the preeminent source of long-term official finance and policy advice for developing countries. One of its major functions is to finance infrastructures such as roads and power facilities and to invest in people by expanding opportunities for education, health care, and housing, and by emphasizing agriculture and rural development.

Community College Outreach: India

I first went to India in 1978 on a short-term Fulbright assignment and returned in 1981, again to serve as a consultant to Indian educators who were considering ways to add vocational and technical components to their institutions. Indian educators have also come to the United States, sponsored by the Fulbright Commission. Since 1982, there has been each year a delegation of about six administrators who have toured U.S. institutions of higher education, mainly community colleges.

A good example of how such exchanges of international visits affect institutional development is provided by a letter and press clipping I received from the dean of colleges of Delhi University. In his letter, the dean said that the clipping "gives an inkling of our efforts in restructuring our courses at the undergraduate level to suit the requirements of the community. I must say my visit to the community colleges in your country, brief as it was, did help in these efforts." Relevant excerpts from the clipping, titled "Delhi University Promoting Job-Oriented Courses" (Singh, 1988, p. 4) follows:

> The University of Delhi has emerged as a pioneer in the field of vocationalizing education. . . . It is the only university which has introduced courses like computer science, electronics, industrial chemistry, agrochemicals and pest control, among others, at the general college level, as opposed to the technical institutions, which cater specially to these subjects only. This "experimentation in job orientation" has affected the education system in another way also—as it has made the system "flexible"—due to the interdisciplinary nature of the courses, the students are offered a wider spectrum to choose from. The acceptance of the new system by the students made the university authorities decide that all new colleges would be based on this pattern alone.

Reflections and Projections

Reflecting on the progress of foreign technical-assistance programs in the community college, it is now hard to believe that very few such programs existed more than ten to fifteen years ago. These changes, as we have suggested earlier, occurred because of changes in the world and changes in the ways in which most leaders of community colleges and others now perceive how our colleges should relate to new international conditions.

Looking ahead, we can anticipate that foreign technical-assistance programs will become an integral part of our colleges. We in the United States should help developing countries because of our greater economic wealth and educational resources. But such involvement also helps us. At the national level, we benefit when the people of our country become better informed and contribute to worldwide economic development and stability. At the community college level, we benefit by enabling our colleges and colleagues to participate in cooperative projects that enhance our own student, faculty, institutional, and community development.

The experience of community colleges in international projects is, relatively speaking, brief. In the future such projects will expand in duration and magnitude. We who have helped cause such effects appreciate the opportunities of working with international colleagues and the compliment such work shows us. We welcome future challenges and confidently believe that our partnership will be of service not only to those directly involved but also to the many others who will eventually benefit from what we are able jointly to accomplish.

Additional Sources

Central American Scholarship Program, P.O. Box 2298, Georgetown University, Washington, D.C. 20057.

Educational Innovation Systems International, P.O. Box 1030, 820 Wisconsin Street, Walworth, Wisconsin 53184.

Training Division of General Electric Corporation, Route 38, Cherry Hill, New Jersey 08358.

The World Bank, 1818 H Street, N.W., Washington, D.C. 20433.

References

Breuder, R. L., and King, M. C. "A Cooperative in the World Community." *Community and Junior College Journal*, 1979, 49 (6), 24–27.
Fersh, S., and Humphrys, J. G. "Caribbean Conference: Mid-Level Manpower Technical/Vocational Training Projects." Cocoa, Fla.: Brevard Community College, 1982.

Harper, W. A. "Trip to Taiwan." *Community and Junior College Journal,* 1980, 51 (3), 16–22.
Moran, T. H. "The International Dimension of Training for Careers." Washington, D.C.: School of Foreign Service, Georgetown University, 1988.
Singh, M. "Delhi University Promoting Job-Oriented Courses." *Times of India,* New Delhi, March 7, 1988, p. 4.

Maxwell C. King is president of Brevard Community College of Cocoa, Florida. In 1976, he became the founding chairman of the board of directors of the Community Colleges for International Development and still serves in that position.

Institutional commitment and adequate resources are needed to provide
effective support services for foreign students in community colleges.

Effective Support Services
for International Students

Martin J. Tillman

In hundreds of cities and campuses across the country, international students represent a significant human resource in the effort to widen the world views of American students and local citizens. Community colleges, with their unique mission and role, have a special contribution to make in shaping the perception and understanding of our society which these students will carry home and share with their peers, family, and friends. The challenge is that, although the student has obviously entered the college to fulfill practical degree requirements, the institution may have the additional expectation of providing a variety of extra-curricular options to bring the student into greater contact and communication with Americans and the local community. This chapter will discuss how well community colleges meet the needs of international, or foreign, students and the kinds of support services required to effectively help them complete their academic sojourn.

Although there are about the same number of international students attending community colleges (46,000, or 13 percent of the 350,000 such students attending all educational institutions according to *Open Doors: 1987–88/1978–79* [Zikopoulos, 1987]) now as a decade ago, a more sophisticated and professional effort has emerged with respect to the design and implementation of support services. Have community colleges kept pace with this trend? Have they committed sufficient resources to the task of training staff and "internationalizing" the campus?

Student Services and Institutional Realities

The difficulties of establishing a cluster of support services to serve the international student should not be underestimated. However, an institution with a clear set of priorities about the role of international educational activities in the context of undergraduate education is more likely to develop effective support services than one that views international education as a frill or as lying on the fringe of the "real" mission of the college. While one might assume that the presence of international students on a campus implies that there is clear and unambiguous commitment to facilitating their entry into the life of the college and the community, recent research does not support this contention. In fact, the very opposite appears to be the norm for community colleges.

Two surveys (of a sample including both two- and four-year colleges) illustrate the contradictory messages sent by campuses enrolling international students. Goodwin and Nacht (1983) found that

- Most academic officials (among those interviewed) place the foreign student low on their list of priorities
- Most institutions have not thought through the economic, educational, political, and organizational issues associated with the presence of large numbers of foreign students on their campuses
- The "humanist presumption" that the foreign student population represents an educational and social presence on campus needs to be supported with stronger evidence.

Seeming to support a link between institutional commitment and clear goal-setting strategies for international education, McCann (1985) states that "In many institutions, foreign student services have not kept pace with student increases over the years [Note: Refers to the period 1981–1985]." Furthermore, his survey also found that two-thirds of the institutions reporting indicated that the decline in service' was due to fiscal constraints; however, of this group, 25 *percent believed that the decline in services to international students was due to a lack of interest in foreign students' problems* (my emphasis).

The most recent study of international educational activities at community colleges, conducted by Anderson for the American Council on Education (1988), confirms the apparent reality of piecemeal approaches (where they exist at all) to development of support services to international students. In his survey of 1,300 colleges, he found that

- Only 38 percent (500) of the colleges reported that they have an administrator responsible for one or more kinds of international educational activities
- Of this group, 77 percent reported that the duties of the administrator include foreign-student services, but, of this group of colleges, 82 percent stated that the administrator so designated to manage these services is doing so on a part-time basis.

It appears that the overall picture at community colleges that enroll international students is not one which is conducive to the development of a pattern of support services that could be characterized as effective. Although there are well-known examples of exemplary institutional commitments, they would appear, in light of the above data, to be few and far between for the majority of institutions.

This points to the question of ethical practices and professional standards with respect to the enrollment of international students. It is possible to provide nominal or ad hoc arrangements of support services for foreign students with part-time staff and without any clear institutional goals with respect to the part the presence of foreign students plays in a broader pattern of international educational activities. However, such practices may not provide the optimal environment in which to enrich the educational experience of both American and international students. In an effort to encourage self-regulation and to provide a set of guidelines for professionals in the field of international education and exchange, the National Association for Foreign Student Affairs (NAFSA) in 1983 established a set of "Principles for International Educational Exchange." Among their guidelines— against which an institution may judge the effectiveness of its scope and pattern of support services for international students—are the following principles:

- The host institution should state clearly its intentions to provide special services for the foreign students and scholars it brings to its campus.
- Regardless of the number of foreign students and scholars, the level of funding, or other circumstances, there *must be one unit in the host institution that is responsible for coordinating these services and there should be a clear and acknowledged designation of responsibility for these services* (my emphasis).
- The institution should provide ample and fully accessible professional services to foreign students and scholars in order *to assure that maximum benefits are derived from the educational experience* (my emphasis).

Organization and Coordination of Support Services

Although the majority of community colleges utilize part-time staff to coordinate their support services for international students, this does not mitigate the responsibility to respond to their needs. Usually, this responsibility falls to a staff person designated as the "foreign-student adviser." Others may use the name "coordinator of international student affairs" or "director of international education." The latter title obviously would indicate a broader mandate to coordinate a wider array of activities which might include study-abroad programs and faculty exchange. As the NAFSA guidelines indicate, the essential standard is to have an identified administrator, preferably working out of a special office, whose responsibility is to provide services that will maximize the educational experience of the international student.

The foreign-student adviser, or FSA, according to Woolston (1983), must carry out many functions; she groups them as follows:

- Administration of the foreign-student advising office
- Consultation and advisement with faculty and staff
- Development of programs
- Participation in academic-guidance programs
- Coordination of financial aid
- Fulfillment of immigration requirements
- Advising and counselling
- Coordination of community relations
- Development and support of student activities
- Maintenance of liaison with nonuniversity agencies
- Coordination of response to emergencies
- Provision for personal services.

These catch-all groupings represent the optimal array of services coordinated by a foreign-student adviser. Of course, it is clear that a part-time person could not effectively perform all these functions. Which should be a priority? Regardless of whether they are performed by one or a number of offices on campus, international students, at one time or another during the course of their academic program, will have needs in one or more of these categories—and the institution must be prepared to respond.

The specific nature and scope of tasks performed by an FSA in a given category follow the phases of a student's sojourn in the United States and can be separated as follows: arrival in the United States, arrival on campus, pursuit of studies, and preparation for return home. With funding from the Office of International Training of the U.S. Agency for International Development, NAFSA has published an excellent pamphlet geared to explaining the role of the foreign-student adviser to the foreign student. It is called "The International Students Office: An Important Resource on Campus." With NAFSA's permission, the following is a summary of the pamphlet (with my emendation and the addition of the first heading):

1. Arrival in the United States. It is the author's judgment that one of the most underestimated points of anxiety and confusion for international students is their arrival at the airport on entry into the United States. Few institutions adequately attempt to portray the complexity of managing the logistics of a major international terminal. With little working knowledge of English and having completed a long flight, students are easily overwhelmed by the situation at customs and in the terminal. They may also be taken advantage of by unscrupulous vendors and taxi drivers. An effective way to ensure the safe arrival of international students is for the FSA and the institution to utilize the Arrival Program service sponsored by the YMCA International Student Service (ISS) with the support and cooperation of the U.S. Information Agency and its Division of Student Support Services. The service is free to students and scholars and operates year-round (including holiday periods). When the FSA or the admissions office sends out the I-20 immigration form, included is a small Arrival Information Request Form (A.I.R.). The student just mails the A.I.R. form back to the ISS office and is assured that an ISS airport representative will meet his or her flight on arrival (the service is available in 14 major cities). This service is deemed important enough that all U.S. Information Agency Overseas Advisers stationed at 366 centers around the world advise students about this service (and also have posters advertising the service). Active support for the Arrival Program by an FSA is perhaps the best way to assure a smooth and safe entry into the U.S. and on to the campus. (For details write: YMCA International Student Service/Arrival Program, 356 W. 34th Street, New York, New York 10001.)

   2. Arrival on Campus.
   Housing
      Maintenance of off-campus housing options
      Provision for meal contract, as appropriate.
   Enrollment
      Requirements for registration, English-language competency testing, acquisition of health insurance, and other procedures
      Immigration regulations and requirements
      Personal assistance with registration and admission process, if necessary.
   Academic Program
      Review of educational objectives and course requirements
      Review of English-language requirements
      Development of orientation covering topics such as the role of FSA office, role of community organizations, role of academic adviser, unique features of U.S. higher education, process for registration, personal concerns.
   Campus Activities
      Orientation to campus events and organizations
      Special social events
      Visits to campus facilities and offices.
   Community Activities
      Homestay with local families
      Orientation to local community services
      Field trips to cultural and recreational sites.
   Personal Concerns
      Culture shock and homesickness

Health services

Immigration and visa matters

Liaison with host government or sponsor

Legal matters.

3. Pursuit of Studies.

Academic Program

Review of academic progress

Review of sponsor relationship, if appropriate

Special needs for remedial services.

Campus Activities

Advising organizations for students of particular nationalities, international clubs, departments

Special cultural events and intercultural programs.

Community Activities

Off-campus enrichment programs with service groups, clubs, religious organizations, and schools

Maintenance of on-going relations with host families

Spouse programs

Special options for vacation travel and national hospitality programs.

Personal Concerns

Adjustment to U.S. society and educational process

Special assistance for medical or legal emergencies

Financial problems; sources of financial assistance

Marital or family problems

Certifications of enrollment for matters such as the transfer of funds or deferral of military requirements.

Immigration

Advising and monitoring of regulations and requirements concerning extension of stay permits, school transfers, visas, passports, work permission, visits abroad, and so forth.

Taxes

Referral to federal and state internal revenue service offices and advice concerning appropriate forms.

4. Preparation for Return Home.

Academic Program

Advice on arrangements for final stages of study, such as need for short-term extensions

Pre-departure details required by U.S. government or sponsor.

Campus Activities

Pre-departure seminars and workshops

Verification of records.

Personal Concerns

Financial problems affecting departure

Travel arrangements

Employment options in home country
Career and vocational plans
Readjustment to home culture, family, and friends.
Immigration
Final requirements regarding status, tax regulations, and so forth.

With limited staff time, a campus would have to pool many of its resources available to all students in order to meet the above needs of international students. For this to occur, there would still have to be additional training of campus personnel to sensitize them to cultural differences and to any special needs of a particular national group. Academic counsellors, support staff, and campus police would benefit from such cross-cultural training or workshops. I would also single out librarians as a special resource group who have daily contact with international students and need to exercise care in their interaction with them. Certainly, one should not presume that faculty possess more or less skill in interacting with international students, although their role is critical to the overall success of the students' experience on campus. I would involve and encourage faculty participation in all campus programs concerning international students. This is all the more likely to occur if faculty are tied to a broad infusion of international educational activity throughout the curriculum and in the community.

Program Development and Professional Resources

For an institution to fulfill its role to educate and fully integrate the foreign student into the life of the campus and surrounding community, the foreign-student adviser and support staff must work toward a set of outcomes beyond the mere execution of administrative tasks. The presence of international students presents numerous opportunities to create an exciting climate of cross-cultural learning that deepens formal classroom work and enriches extracurricular programming.

Programs of enrichment for the international student will have more meaningful and fewer improvised outcomes if goals are developed to meet both the academic and personal needs of students. An outline for such a set of programs appears in Table 1. This schema was the outgrowth of the author's participation in a national conference held at the Wingspread Conference Center in 1985 and sponsored by NAFSA and the Johnson Foundation. The theme was "Programming for Change." The premise of these discussions was that the more improvised and unplanned the programs for international students, the less likely it was that the programs would have beneficial long-term effects on either the campus community or the international student. Given the short period of time the international student spends at the community college, it would seem both logical and prudent to maximize the benefits of staff time and outlay of institutional resources on their behalf.

Table 1. Programming International Students on Campus

Objective	Fostering Interaction Between U.S. International Students	Aiding Adjustment	Community Outreach	Education of Campus Officials	Fostering Awareness of Global Issues and Social Concerns	Recreation/ Entertainment
Social/Cultural	Coffee houses International living centers Field trips	Coffee houses International centers Wives' programs Field trips Host-family program	Talent shows International fairs Host-family program Nationality nights			Talent shows Fairs Nationality nights Films, dances Coffee hours
Educative	Field trips Wives' programs	Study-skill workshops Career development workshops Peer assistance Host-family program	Speakers' bureau Field trips Host-family program Public school discussions	Re-entry seminar	Forums Speakers' bureau Development education seminars	
Service	Internships		Community service projects		Public school discussions Speakers' bureau	

Listed below is an array of professional resources available to assist the adviser and other professionals and staff who work with international students. These materials, training programs, and grants are invaluable tools to strengthen and broaden support services, build programs, and facilitate the professional development of staff. (See Chapter Ten in this volume for a discussion of linkages and networks with community groups.)

American Association of Community and Junior Colleges, One Dupont Circle, Washington, D.C. 20036.
Through the office of the director of international education, special contracts are negotiated (currently with Honduras and China) for placing students on a campus in partnership with a sister institution in the host country. The office monitors the performance of students and serves as the liaison to the embassy.

Institute of International Education, 809 United Nations Plaza, New York, New York 10017.
IIE has created a new ad hoc committee of community college representatives to ensure widespread dissemination of its literature and research reports and to widen access to its related professional programs. Regional offices across the United States can offer assistance in enrichment programs and involvement of Fulbright scholars in classroom programs or faculty seminars. International visitors sponsored by the U.S. Information Agency may also be programmed to go to a college to discuss technical and vocational programs and other aspects of the curriculum. IIE also maintains overseas advising centers in China, Hong Kong, Mexico, and Thailand. A new national survey is underway to develop a community-college data base on available resources for managing short-term training contracts (for example, with the Agency for International Development). Over 550 institutions are part of their Educational Associates network and receive important publications, including *Open Doors* and reports on the status of international students and trends in providing services.

U.S. Information Agency, Office of Advising, Teaching and Specialized Programs, 301 4th Street, S.W., Washington, D.C. 20547.
This division of the USIA provides grant support for publications, services, and professional development to key agencies and organizations serving international students. Their 366 overseas educational advising centers are provided educational materials, including descriptions of the community college system. Included is the new video, "If You Want to Study in the USA," which outlines the entry process and requirements to academic institutions. USIA supports the training activities of the NAFSA Field Service Program, the College Board, and the YMCA/ISS Arrival Program for airport reception. Overseas advisers who participate in the annual U.S.-based training program may also be invited to visit community colleges.

The College Entrance Examination Board, Office of International Education, 1717 Massachusetts Ave., N.W., Washington, D.C. 20036.

The College Entrance Examination Board publishes very useful and informative brochures including *Financial Planning for Study in the United States, Entering Higher Education in the United States, Guidelines for the Recruitment of Foreign Students,* and the *Director of Overseas Educational Advising Centers.* Also valuable, and new, is the *College Handbook Foreign Student Supplement: 1987–88,* which provides an excellent overview of the process for selection and application to an American college (this could be useful in the development of pre-arrival materials and on-campus orientation). Noteworthy is their Foreign Student Information Clearinghouse, which provides a data base of information supplied by colleges to assist students overseas to review and select a college that matches their academic and personal interests.

National Association for Foreign Student Affairs, 1860 19th Street, N.W., Washington, D.C. 20009.

NAFSA membership is essential to maintain links to new developments in the field of international education and support services for international students. Their professional resources are varied and relate to every area of concern to the FSA and support staff. Publications and training relate to special sections, including community volunteers and programs (COMSEC, or Community Section), admissions (ADSEC, or Admissions Section), English as a second language (TESOL, or Association of Teachers of English as a Second Language), and foreign-student advising (CAFSS, or Council of Advisers to Foreign Students and Scholars). NAFSA consultants are available to advise and review efforts to improve support services. In addition, noteworthy resources include publications and training and program grants, which are described below.

• Publications: CAFSS Bibliography (revised edition) (1988); Guideline Series, on such topics as foreign-student finances, admissions, and orientation; *Teaching Across Cultures in the University ESL Program; Learning Across Cultures; Faculty Member's Guide to U.S. Immigration Law; Crisis Management in a Cross-Cultural Setting; Private Sector Funding Available to Foreign Scholars and Students in the United States; Programs for Spouses of Foreign Students; Teaching English as a Second Language—A Guide for the Volunteer Teacher; The Profession of Foreign Student Advising; Friendship with a Foreign Student and Friendship with Your American Host.* (Note: This is only a partial listing.)

• Training and Program Grants: With support from USIA, NAFSA offers an array of options through its field-service office that can enhance the services and professionalism of campus support-staff. Grants are awarded to professionals at different levels of their careers—newcomers and mid- or senior-level staff—for site visits and staff exchanges. Grants are awarded to attend training programs and seminars. Other awards are for conference travel, development of regional workshops, and research.

The NAFSA/Agency for International Development Committee awards a variety of research grants to investigate issues such as the special needs of students from developing nations who are involved in short-term technical training programs in the United States. Also, in conjunction with the AACJC International Consortium, special training workshops aimed at strengthening international-student support services were funded in the 1988–1989 academic year. The Cooperative Grants Program (COOP) encourages the development of innovative programs that foster the involvement on and off campus of the foreign student. This program has been under-utilized by community colleges in recent years. (Only five grants were awarded to two-year institutions between 1985 and 1988.) Grants are available in such areas as community and host-family programs, international students as campus resources, international classroom programs, cultural adjustment and orientation, and international career development and practical training.

Conclusion

The development of effective support services for international students is tied to the commitment of the college to an overall strategy and set of clear goals in support of international educational activities. Most community colleges that enroll international students have many constraints. Most colleges do not assign full-time staff to perform the duties of advising foreign students, and there are institutions that care little for their needs. The special advantages that community colleges have for foreign students are undermined if the institution commits only the minimum resources to their welfare and educational goals. Ironically, a growing array of professional services and resources aimed at strengthening campus support-services is available. There is also growing interest in utilizing community colleges as a base for short-term technical training projects for students from developing nations.

Such projects and training grants for staff, coupled with creative linkages to community groups and voluntary agencies, can expand the learning experiences of all students, faculty, and local citizens. Institutions must be ready and willing to build a climate that embraces the opportunities that result from bringing international students to campus. Effective support services serve more than the short-term needs of these students; they open a window to learning from and about people and cultures beyond the borders of the campus and community.

References

American Council on Education. *Foreign Students and Institutional Policy: Toward an Agenda for Action.* Washington, D.C.: American Council on Education, 1982.

Anderson, C. J. *International Studies and Undergraduates: 1987.* American Council on Education Higher Education Report, no. 76. Washington, D.C.: American Council on Education, 1988.

College Entrance Examination Board. *The Foreign Student in U.S. Community and Junior Colleges.* New York: College Entrance Examination Board, 1978.

Goodwin, C. D., and Nacht, M. *Absence of Decision: Foreign Students in American Colleges and Universities.* New York: Institute of International Education, 1983.

Lee, M. Y., and others. *Needs of Foreign Students from Developing Nations at U.S. Colleges and Universities.* Washington, D.C.: National Association for Foreign Student Affairs, 1981.

McCann, W. J. *A Survey of Policy Changes: Foreign Students in Public Institutions of Higher Education from 1983 to 1985.* New York: Institute of International Education, 1986.

National Association for Foreign Student Affairs. "The International Students Office: An Important Resource on Campus." Washington, D.C.: National Association for Foreign Student Affairs, 1983a.

National Association for Foreign Student Affairs. *NAFSA Principles for International Educational Exchange.* Washington, D.C.: National Association for Foreign Student Affairs, 1983b.

Tillman, M. "The Partnership of Voluntary Organizations and American Higher Education Institutions in Developing Enrichment Opportunities for International Students." Unpublished manuscript, 1987.

Woolston, V. "Administration: Coordinating and Integrating Programs and Services." In H. M. Jenkins and Associates, *Educating Students from Other Nations: American Colleges and Universities in International Educational Interchange.* San Francisco: Jossey-Bass, 1983.

Zikopoulos, M. (ed.). *Open Doors: 1987/88. Report on International Educational Exchange.* New York: Institute of International Education, 1987.

Martin J. Tillman is director of International Education Services for Legacy International in Alexandria, Virginia. Earlier, he was associate director of YMCA International Program Services and director of the International Student Service from 1984 to 1987.

*On-campus and off-campus programs should be linked to provide
for more effective learning for foreign and U.S. students in U.S.
colleges.*

Developing the Campus-Community Link in International Education

Gail A. Hochhauser

There is a need to "internationalize" international education. Rather than
only learn about other nations and cultures, students need also to learn
from them. This holds true both for foreign students and scholars on U.S.
college campuses and for U.S. students and faculty. One way to help this to
occur is to effectively integrate international students and scholars into the
learning process, both inside and outside the classroom. While recognizing
that the primary purpose of study and research abroad is to obtain a
degree or to further develop professional skills, educational institutions
have an obligation to help foreign students take advantage of the varied
programs of campus and community-based intercultural involvement available to them throughout their period of academic study. Indeed, colleges
and universities should take on the role of resource centers and should act
as catalysts in bringing international students into closer touch with community groups. Just as student life is not automatically broadened by the
interaction of students from different cultures, community contacts should
be above the level of strictly business and economic exchanges, as of a
grocery store clerk with a customer.

This chapter looks at on-campus and off-campus programs. (Most of
these programs are considered "non-academic" but that means only that
they take place primarily outside the classroom, not that the student does
not learn.) It will use a nuts-and-bolts approach in describing ways to
encourage cooperative efforts between faculty and foreign students. And it
will offer practical suggestions for campus-community outreach activities,

including using international students, scholars, and visitors as resources in the community, and ways to locate resource people in the community for campus-based international programs. It is important to note that there is no ideal situation. The ideal for an institution is the program that works best, given the institution's history, staff, goals, and resources.

On the Campus

The office of international education should serve to communicate, coordinate, and facilitate enrichment opportunities for international students. A problem to overcome in the campus community is that extracurricular activities using international students are seen by many in an academic environment as ancillary in nature and not necessary or vital to the education of the student. These activities are viewed as fine to the extent that they do not intrude on the educational process or on the university budget. Goodwin and Nacht, in the 1983 study *Absence of Decision: Foreign Students in American Colleges and Universities,* pointed to the general indifference to international students by U.S. institutions, especially as manifested by the lack of special programs and support services for such students. State legislatures also usually do not consider international programs and activities essential components of a college. Competition for diminishing national grants may also discourage support from sympathetic faculty, as will the lack of a reward system within the institution's promotion and tenure process that would recognize the contributions made by faculty to outreach extracurricular programs. In the short run, then, it may be the dedication and hard work of a few staff members that will provide success for outreach programs with little or no funding. But in the long run, either funding must be found, or the volunteer base must be expanded to include personnel outside the advising office.

It is important here to note some differences between community colleges and four-year institutions, which must be considered in establishing both on-campus and community-based programs for international students.

• Most community colleges do not have resident dormitories. Students commute to campus and live off-campus in private housing. Therefore the use of international houses or dorms to bring U.S. and foreign students together in a common living place is not a possibility.

• There is a difference between foreign students at community colleges and their U.S. peers in the time they spend on campus. Most U.S. students enrolled at community colleges are part time. They may attend school for four years or more before obtaining a degree. International students, on student visas, are required to be full-time students. It will be a challenge to involve the commuting, part-time U.S. student in activities after class hours. It will also be a challenge to provide opportunities that will reach out to the nontraditional student on campus, specifically the adult student and the occasional student.

• Relatively few community colleges have the extent of support systems for international activities that many four-year institutions have. The international student adviser's office may be open only certain hours, for example, and be staffed on a part-time basis.

Types of Activities. Activities on campus using foreign students, scholars, and returned U.S. students include:

• International Days—special programs, films, international affairs discussions, and so on, focusing on a particular geographic area.

• International Students Association (or Club)—a student organization promoting cultural learning and interaction between U.S. and foreign students, with activities such as dances, music festivals, and the like.

• Study Abroad Fairs—featuring international students, U.S. students, visiting faculty, and U.S. faculty who have traveled and worked abroad.

• Foreign-student peer advising—both informal helping of students by students and more formal activities where foreign students and culturally sensitive U.S. students assist foreign students who are having academic or social problems. Remember that foreign students on campus encompass not only traditional exchange students but also children of graduate and postgraduate foreign students, diplomats, foreign businessmen, military personnel, refugees, and so on.

• English-language tutoring programs—interesting for American students who have returned from foreign-study programs.

• Credit-bearing and noncredit seminars, symposia, conferences, and so on—good ways to draw in the adult education and lifelong learning constituencies on campus. Informality should be promoted, as an open style and setting encourages candor in sharing information. Opportunities for social mingling also increase openness.

• Pre-departure orientation programs for U.S. students and faculty going abroad—using foreign students and scholars as resources.

Funding. International education does not receive a large amount of funding from private and public sources. Rather, administrators often have to deal with minimal funding and little more than moral support and occasional encouragement. The reality is that most money for these enrichment programs will be "soft money," and offices may be in a constant search for dollars to maintain an activity.

To meet the funding challenge and still be a success in programming for international students, offices can take creative approaches to building their cases on campus. The international education office should cooperate with other offices and departments on campus, including the Continuing Education and Business departments. If funding for enrichment activities cannot be found in the international education office's budget, perhaps other offices on campus— the Student Activities Office, for example—might supply some funding.

One way to reduce costs is to share resources with other local institutions. An example is to cosponsor the training of foreign students as peer and U.S. student advisers and as speakers in the community. Another example is to cooperate in inviting speakers, sharing the expense of fees, and so on. Yet a third example is putting together a television series on international affairs, cosponsored by several institutions. A number of schools might cooperatively apply for grants to do such things as surveys of the community resources for global education.

The International Visitor Program of the U.S. Information Agency (USIA) provides funding for members of group projects as well as individuals to visit cities and regions appropriate to specific professional areas. These visitors are here as private citizens and do not expect special ceremonies or to be involved in protocol. Professional programs, which are designed prior to the trip abroad, include appointments with U.S. colleagues and counterparts, sightseeing, attendance at cultural events, home stays, and so on. Visitors who speak English travel alone; escorts are usually provided for those whose English is not fluent.

The U.S. college campus, as well as local community sponsors, will be contacted either directly by USIA or by one of the private agencies (such as the Institute of International Education or the African-American Institute), which, under a USIA contract, are responsible for programming international visitors, to set up appointments and to provide hospitality. If a campus agrees to participate in a visit, it will be responsible for details of the visitor's program as it relates to interests on the campus vis-à-vis the international visitor. The campus contributes its time and hospitality on a voluntary basis. The visitor's travel and per-diem costs are paid for by the USIA program.

Community colleges are a good resource for international visitors, who are often mid-career-level professionals in fields traditionally taught at the community college. Educators are also USIA visitors. Campuses interested in being considered as hosts for these visitors should contact USIA and the nationally based program agencies. In any discussion that follows such contacts, emphasize areas of particular strength on campus and be prepared to discuss expertise of staff and faculty, courses and curriculum, and related technical and vocational programs that would be of interest to a particular international visitor. Having international visitors on campus is a wonderful way to develop future international contacts. It is a chance to build an institution's image in the international arena. And these visits provide an infusion of an international perspective on the campus and the surrounding community.

Off-Campus Linkages to the Community

The aim of campus-community programs is twofold. One is to use the resources of the community to facilitate the academic progress and personal development of international students and scholars. The second is to use these students and scholars to strengthen the international dimension of the community.

The impetus for developing a community outreach program can come from the campus. An administrator, someone with skills to exercise professional leadership in the community, needs to identify people in the community who can also attract others to the program. Effective administrators involve not only volunteers from the community but also university staff and students in designing programs. In this way, all these groups are committed to the program's success and continuation.

The linkages between campus and community are many. Colleges are part of the social and economic fabric of the community. (The tightness of the bond will vary depending on whether the college is in a small or large city and whether the institution is large enough to dominate the economic, social, and cultural life of the community.) Faculty and students serve in a wide range of leadership positions throughout the community. Institutions of higher education often serve as partners with business to enhance economic development in the community, and additional linkages to the business community involving international education can provoke different perspectives on issues and lead to the development of joint services that draw on campus and community resources.

The internationalization of community resources can be viewed as part of the growing trend toward continuing education and lifelong learning, concepts increasingly important today as communities require outreach programs from their local institutions of higher education. Increased communication can also promote better understanding of educational needs, which can lead to greater public support of the educational institution.

Community-based human resources are easily found. Volunteer potential exists in community groups such as the following: university alumni; business and professional groups, including representatives of foreign firms and multinational businesses; ethnic groups; churches and synagogues; parent groups at local public and parochial schools; Peace Corps returnees; retired foreign-service officers; retired military personnel; scouting groups; representatives of foreign institutions and organizations; and others. Look around the community for meetings of such public-education organizations as the United Nations Association, the League of Women Voters, the Foreign Policy Association, the Society for International Development, world-trade councils of chambers of commerce, labor groups, and political committees.

Types of Activities. The types of activities vary. While some are specific to a particular community interest group, others are general and open to all interested people on campus and in the community.

The international student office can sponsor programs for the community—workshops on such topics as cross-cultural perspectives on current events or lectures combining foreign students and scholars and their

U.S. counterparts. A Speakers' Bureau is an activity by which members of the community or faculty members who wish to introduce a comparative approach to their constituency may request international students as guest lecturers. A Great Decisions Program, based on materials produced by the Foreign Policy Association, can use, as resources, international students and faculty as well as members of the community. Foreign students might also be interested in volunteer service projects in the community. Other examples of activities linking international students and the community include the following: a Global Week, during which a major issue is examined from an international perspective and international students are encouraged to participate, giving their perspectives gained from living and studying abroad; intercultural workshops for elementary and secondary school students and their teachers, using international students as resources; K–12 teacher-training programs, including in-service courses on some aspect of a particular foreign culture, or development of curriculum materials; international food fairs, craft demonstrations, music programs, fashion shows, and similar activities.

The campus adviser should also look at developments in the community to help foster international-program events. For example, the growth of international business activities in the community can result in resources providing consultants and speakers. Some financial support may also be forthcoming by way of linkages with community businesses, in the form of workshops and conferences developed and held for the business community or through innovative foreign-language courses developed for businessmen and travelers. The institution can work with the state's department of commerce to provide services for visits by foreign business and industry leaders. Such linkages can also provide opportunities for internships for international students and advice on international careers for U.S. students. A calendar of upcoming international events in the community should be publicized. Be creative. Advisers in New York, for example, used international-student volunteers to help interpret for foreign athletes at the New York City Marathon.

Contacts outside the classroom are, of course, an excellent way for international students to gain exposure to American culture, to practice English, and have a positive cross-cultural experience. Many institutions have home-hospitality programs whereby international students have an opportunity to visit with American families, usually for an evening and dinner. Hosts can be people in a professional area of particular interest to the foreign student or people who simply want to meet someone from another country and culture. Local host families can involve international students in a variety of other activities, including vacation hospitality, observations of national holidays, visits to community businesses, general sightseeing, shopping assistance, English-language programs, and so on. Two Washington, D.C.-based organizations, the National Council for International Visitors (NCIV) and the Community Section of the National Association for Foreign Student Affairs (NAFSA), can work with colleges in helping to set up a host-family program.

Community volunteers, particularly host families, can be invaluable in providing emotional and logistical support for foreign students. Many volunteers are as professional and committed to international exchange as campus professionals.

Funding. Funding for outreach programs is a problem; it may be difficult just getting sufficient money to start new programs and to establish community contacts.

The U.S. Agency for International Development (AID) has awarded some institutions seed money for projects with the theme "(name of city or state) in the World Economy." These are basically public awareness projects organized by college personnel and representatives of local businesses and community leaders to expand the public's understanding of international economic issues. Conferences, with topics such as the impact of international trade and investment, or the ethnic makeup of a community, are an example of the type of activity funded.

NAFSA's Cooperative Grants Program (COOP) accepts proposals for projects semi-annually. COOP grants, among other things, support the development of innovative programming to enrich the experience of foreign students attending U.S. colleges and universities. The program is funded through a grant from the U.S. Information Agency (USIA). NAFSA also awards Community Strengthening Grants, which go to organizations working with foreign students and scholars in the community. These grants, made possible through funding by USIA, are intended to aid organizations that have a strong track record in providing services to international students and scholars but that are currently struggling to meet those needs.

Other possible sources of income include corporate contributions and fees from activities, including participant fees.

Visibility in the community is crucial to the future health—and support—of campus-community linkages. The use of flyers, public-service announcements on local television and radio stations, and news releases to local newspapers are good ways to publicize and promote activities. The media should also be alerted to the availability of foreign students, scholars, and visitors for interviews and to provide background and briefings to editorial boards.

A good forum for presenting news of international programs, on campus or in the community, is a monthly newsletter. The newsletter can provide a calendar of events and information on lectures and programs on campus as well as locally.

Conclusion

Successful campus-community outreach activities can occur as long as colleges and universities assume the role of catalyst in bringing international students and scholars together with significant on- and off-campus programs. Competition for the small amount of money available for programming, whether from national grants, state funds, or campus allocations, may necessitate the development of a creative volunteer base of campus and community personnel with international interests and commitment to a program's success. There must, however, be some level of commitment throughout the institution to conduct these enrichment programs. For such programs to succeed, support for them should come from the office of the college's president.

Help in locating community resources, both for potential volunteers as well as programming opportunities, can be found in a variety of places. This includes the programs of a number of national associations. USIA-sponsored international visitors, for example, are a good means of providing infusion of an international perspective on campus. Resources on as well as off campus can support the international mission of an institution.

An inventory of existing campus resources that would support campus-community linkages is a needed first step for anyone interested in setting up such an activity. The inventory can identify strengths as well as weaknesses, point out areas that need additional work, and provide a basis for funding requirements and personnel needs. Some questions to consider in developing such an inventory are the following:

- Is there a clearly articulated institutional policy that recognizes the importance of campus and community linkages and that clearly details campus commitment of funds and personnel for related activities?

- Who coordinates campus-community linkages? Is there a core of interested faculty or administrators able to work in this area? Does the institution have financial resources to support these people, or will efforts, at least initially, be strictly on a voluntary basis?

- What efforts are currently underway to internationalize the campus environment through lectures, foreign visitors, cultural programming, and so on? Are foreign students provided with opportunities for extracurricular or cocurricular activities? Does the institution provide U.S. students and faculty who have studied or worked abroad with opportunities to share and integrate their overseas experiences and insights in a an organized way?

- Is there information readily available on community resources, including the location of multinational businesses, civic and religious organizations, retired people with international interests, and home stay and community hospitality volunteers? What is the best way to access this information? What are the expectations of community resources in campus linkages? How can community resources be used to enrich the institution's international goals?

- Has the institution made efforts to contact government and national agencies that might act as funders and resources for building linkages between campus and community? Is the institution willing to cooperate with these outside organizations in various outreach programs? Are there other institutions in the region with international outreach programs, and could these provide possible channels for cooperative ventures?

• Is there a systematic, timely procedure in place for evaluating the effectiveness of campus-community linkages, and is there a way to ensure that such linkages meet the goals of the international mission of the institution?

Finally, there should be the realization that international students and visitors, and the campus of which they are a part, are not the only beneficiaries of enrichment programs. The internationalization of a community—businesses, service industries, civic organizations, and, above all, local citizens—will permit the community to develop and maintain an awareness appropriate to the interdependent world of which it is a part.

Additional Sources

Althen, G. (ed.). *Learning Across Cultures: Intercultural Communication and International Exchange.* Washington, D.C.: National Association for Foreign Student Affairs, 1981.

Goodwin, C., and Nacht, M. *Absence of Decision: Foreign Students in American Colleges and Universities.* New York: Institute of International Education, 1983.

Hjelt, M. C., and Stewart, G. *Teaching English as a Second Language: A Guide for the Volunteer Teacher.* Washington, D.C.: National Association for Foreign Student Affairs, 1986.

Joshi, J., and Hochhauser, G. A. *Human Resources for Global and Development Education.* Washington, D.C.: Consortium for International Cooperation in Higher Education, 1988.

National Association for Foreign Student Affairs. *Handbook for Community Organizations Working with Foreign Students: Developing, Maintaining, Revitalizing Programs.* Washington, D.C.: National Association for Foreign Student Affairs, 1986.

Rhinesmith, S. *Bring Home the World: A Management Guide for Community Leaders of International Exchange Programs.* New York: Walker, 1985.

Reference

Baldassare, M., and Katz, C. *International Exchange Off-Campus: Foreign Students and Local Communities.* New York: Institute of International Education, 1986.

Gail A. Hochhauser is director of the U.S. AID/AASCU Linkages Program of the American Association of State Colleges and Universities, Washington, D.C.

*This chapter provides an annotated bibliography on international
education, including general overviews and materials on curriculum
development, international business education, foreign students, and
international student exchange.*

Sources and Information: Internationalizing the Community College

Ruth I. Cape, Anita Y. Colby

As recently as the early 1980s, most community college presidents and
trustees were far from endorsing international education on their campuses.
However, increased involvement of the United States in the global economy,
growth in the number of foreign students in the United States, and interest
in community colleges by government officials and educators from other
countries have all contributed to increasing recognition of the role that
community colleges can play in international education.

For some colleges, internationalizing the curriculum has meant a revitalization of foreign-language and study-abroad programs. Other colleges
have developed new community-service and academic programs to train
local businesses and entrepreneurs to participate in international trade.
Still others have adopted college-wide interdisciplinary approaches, integrating instructional modules on international or multicultural themes into
existing courses in a wide range of disciplines. As community colleges
continue to internationalize their curricula, accommodate more foreign
students in their classrooms, and engage in technical-assistance projects in
other countries, they find themselves at the very center of major issues in
the field of international education and are able to strengthen the entire
international education enterprise.

The following materials reflect recent literature in the ERIC system on
curriculum development and other aspects of international education. The
full text of ERIC documents can be read on microfiche at over 700 libraries
nationwide or may be ordered from the ERIC Document Reproduction

Service (EDRS) in Alexandria, Virginia (1-800-227-ERIC). For an EDRS form, a list of libraries in your area that house ERIC microfiche collections, or more information about our services, please contact the ERIC Clearinghouse for Junior Colleges, 8118 Math-Sciences Building, University of California, Los Angeles, Ca. 90024 (213-825-3931).

General Overviews

Adams, A. H., and Earwood, G. *Internationalizing the Community College.* ISHE Fellows Program Research Report No. 2. Tallahassee, Fla.: Institute for Studies in Higher Education, 1982. 54 pp. (ED 225 638)
This monograph on community colleges and international and intercultural education emphasizes North American students' low level of awareness of international affairs and events and the importance of a knowledge of other societies in an increasingly interdependent world. After citing various definitions of international education, the monograph examines the role of the community college in the development of such education.

Ebersole, B. J. "International Education: Where and How Does It Fit in Your College?" *Community, Technical, and Junior College Journal,* 1989, 59 (3), 29-31.
This article draws from a study of international education at community colleges to discuss patterns of program administration, financial commitments and expectations, the importance of establishing an institutional policy on international education, and potential problems.

Fersh, S., and Greene, W. (eds.). *The Community College and International Education: A Report of Progress.* Vol. 2. Fort Lauderdale, Fla.: Broward Community College, 1984. 357 pp. (ED 245 736)
Designed to highlight progress made by community colleges in the United States in international education, this report presents a collection of materials representing various state and institutional initiatives and efforts. Part I contains articles that provide a history of the development of the international education movement. Part II contains excerpts from legislation and reports illustrating the progress made in Florida in advancing international education. Part III provides information on projects and programs supported by grants from the United States.

King, M. "Providing Leadership and Implementation for International Education in Community Colleges." Paper presented at the League for Innovation in the Community College Conference, "Leadership 2000," San Francisco, June 11-14, 1989. 12 pp. (ED 307 954)
This paper begins by defining international education as all studies and programs that help students learn about the world beyond their own nation

and transcend their culturally conditioned, ethnocentric perspectives, perceptions, and behavior. The paper goes on to examine the more than a dozen two-year college consortia devoted to international education, financial and information resources provided by a variety of agencies, and exemplary programs at many community colleges. A special focus of the paper is Community Colleges for International Development (CCID), a consortium of forty U.S. and Canadian community colleges established to provide opportunities for international study, exchange, and professional development to two-year college students and faculty and cooperating institutions abroad. CCID colleges' work is highlighted in the areas of long- and short-term education and technical assistance to interested countries.

King, M., and Fersh, S. "International Education and the U.S. Community College: From Optional to Integral." *Junior College Resource Review*, Spring 1983. Los Angeles, Calif.: ERIC Clearinghouse for Junior Colleges. 6 pp. (ED 233 780)
This resource review considers the factors contributing to the increased emphasis on international education in community colleges, highlights some of the programs and cooperative efforts advancing international education, and provides a list of the resources and organizations available to help community colleges implement international education. The review provides information on the growth of foreign enrollments in two-year colleges, the increasing importance of foreign tourists and trade to the U.S. economy, and the implications of technical-assistance and educational-exchange programs for community colleges.

King, M. C., and Fersh, S. H. "International Education: Its Future Is Now." *Community, Technical, and Junior College Journal*, 1989, *59* (3), 28–29.
This article lists resources to help community colleges integrate international education into their programs and services. It identifies consortia concerned with international education and sources of grants and information. It also describes Brevard Community College's (Florida) international education efforts and discusses specific implications for general education.

Nielsen, N. "How a Small/Rural College May Start and Sustain an International Program." Paper presented at the 68th Annual Convention of the American Association of Community and Junior Colleges, Las Vegas, Nev., April 24–27, 1988. 7 pp. (ED 294 643)
This paper lists a variety of ways that community colleges can develop an international education program. The college should examine its reasons for wanting to start an international education program. A college may approach the development of its international program by adding international components to existing courses. After establishing the objectives of

its international program, the college can begin implementing the program by mobilizing the faculty and staff.

Prast, L. L. "International Education: On a Shoestring." *Community, Technical, and Junior College Journal*, 1989, 59 (3), 31–33.
This article describes Delta College's (Michigan) efforts to expand global awareness on campus and encourage international education within a limited budget. These efforts include plaques affixed to classroom doors presenting information on different countries, a foreign-film library, a Peace Corps Partnership Project, a team-taught course on Third World nations, and a Global Awareness Week.

Curriculum Development

Brown, P. A. (ed.). "Internationalizing the Curriculum." Washington, D.C.: Association of American Colleges, 1984. 19 pp. (ED 242 239)
Perspectives on developing international understanding are considered, and descriptions of the international education programs at fifteen colleges and universities are presented. The articles in this collection discuss initiatives to promote international awareness and discuss international programs and their requirements.

Greene, W. "Area 8: The International/Intercultural General Education Requirement." *Community and Junior College Journal*, 1985, 55 (4), 18–23.
This article reviews the President's Commission on Foreign Language and International Studies' recommendations for increasing international and intercultural components of general-education curricula. It describes Broward Community College's (Florida) curriculum development efforts, which resulted in an international-intercultural general education requirement for associate-in-arts students. It also discusses other examples of Broward's commitment to international education.

Harris, M. E. "Internationalizing Curricula: Articulation Between Two- and Four-Year Colleges and Universities." Paper presented at the 25th Annual Convention of the International Studies Association, Atlanta, Ga., March 27–31, 1984. 9 pp. (ED 246 941)
This paper looks at the efforts of two- and four-year college educators in the Pacific Northwest to internationalize the curricula of two-year colleges in the region. The paper highlights the activities of the Northwest International Education Association, a consortium of forty colleges and universities, in the areas of curriculum development and the establishment of direct links with the business community. The consortium has also sponsored training programs, summer institutes, and research programs for two- and four-year college faculty. Drawing from the experience of educa-

tors in the Pacific Northwest, the paper identifies necessary steps to ensure articulation between two- and four-year colleges in the area of international education, including gaining support of college administrators and trustees, applying for grants, involving faculty in articulation discussions, and providing substantive faculty-development programs.

Hendrickson, J. M. "Internationalizing the Community College Curriculum." *Hispania,* 1989, 72 (2), 431–433.
This article suggests that in order to better internationalize their curricula, community colleges should (1) require one academic year of foreign-language study, (2) design foreign-language curricula to develop students' functional proficiency, (3) develop language courses to serve the community's and students' unique foreign-language needs and interests, and (4) strengthen ties with local secondary schools.

King, M. C., and Fersh, S. C. "General Education Through International Intercultural Dimensions." In B. L. Johnson (ed.), *General Education in Two-Year Colleges.* New Directions for Community Colleges, no. 40. San Francisco: Jossey-Bass, 1982.
This article underscores community colleges' responsibility for incorporating an international component in their general education curricula. It assesses the impact of foreign student enrollments, foreign tourists, and global society. It reviews Brevard Community College's (Florida) international-intercultural education programs and stresses the relationships of transcultural education with general education and of faculty development with curriculum development.

Nilles, M. F. "Bringing Home the World: A Case for Internationalizing Curricula." *Community Review,* 1982, 4 (2), 16–21.
This article asserts the need for global education in an increasingly interdependent world. It focuses on reasons colleges should be involved in internationalizing their curricula and suggests several curricular modifications to make English as a Second Language courses more relevant to the future needs of students.

Paquette, W. "Internationalizing the American History Curriculum." Paper presented at the National Conference of the Community College Humanities Association, Washington, D.C., November 9–11, 1989. 21 pp. (ED 312 023)
This paper describes Tidewater Community College's (Virginia) efforts to add an international dimension to the curriculum. The process began in 1988, when twenty faculty members from various disciplines participated in a series of lectures on the culture, history, politics, and economics of China and Japan. One of the goals of the lecture series was to infuse an

international dimension into as many existing courses as possible in all disciplines. One participant developed six units for incorporation into a two-semester American History course. Instruction involved readings in the course textbook and other supplementary sources, map exercises, films, videotapes, guest speakers, and class discussions. In addition, the instructor prepared "Perspective Sheets" listing some of the traditional values held by the culture under consideration during the time period covered in the unit. The paper provides sample "Perspective Sheets" on Chinese and Japanese culture and forty-five references.

Salas, D. J. "Infusing International Experience into the Curriculum." Princeton, N.J.: Princeton University Mid-Career Fellowship Program, 1988. 19 pp. (ED 297 791)

This paper traces New Jersey's Raritan Valley Community College's efforts to increase students' global awareness through the development of a number of courses and programs designed to infuse an international and intercultural perspective into the curriculum. Among the college's on-going projects are an international lecture series offered by on- and off-campus experts in the arts, humanities, and social sciences and faculty-exchange and study-abroad programs during summer and semester breaks.

Tamarkin, T. "Intensive Language Programs: Two Models for the Community College. International Immersion Program." *Hispania*, 1988, 71 (1), 177–179.

This article describes the adaptation of an intensive Spanish-language program to suit the needs of community colleges. Outcomes including increased student enthusiasm and enrollment and more comprehensive coverage of material are cited.

International Business Education

Burmeister-May, S. "A Model International Business Education Program for Small Business." *Proceedings of the Seventh Annual Eastern Michigan University Conference on Languages for Business and the Professions*, Ann Arbor, Mich., April 7–9, 1988. 8 pp. (ED 304 916)

This paper describes Normandale Community College's (Minnesota) efforts to address the community's need for international training for small business. Normandale applied for and obtained a federal grant for a program to assist twenty small to medium-sized firms in increasing their export capabilities to the Netherlands and West Germany. The program is directed primarily toward women- and minority-owned companies and has five training components: (1) six how-to-export workshops, (2) an international marketing seminar series, (3) a small-business export manual, (4) individual consulting services, and (5) training in language and cultural-survival skills.

Fifield, M. L., and Sam, D. F. "Loop College Business and International Education Project." Chicago: Chicago City Colleges, 1986. 13 pp. (ED 269 056)

This document describes the activities undertaken by Loop College (Illinois) under a one-year Title VI Part B, Business and International Education grant. The project was supported by the college and thirty-seven members of the Chicago international business community. Activities included the integration of international perspectives into course content through the addition of modular units to existing courses, the creation of three new international business courses, professional development efforts, and programs to promote interaction between foreign-born and American-born Loop College students.

Fifield, M. L., and Sam, D. F. "International Business Curriculum: The New Impact of Community Colleges." *Community, Technical, and Junior College Journal,* 1989, 59 (3), 36–39.

This article examines several aspects of international business education, including curriculum development, partnerships with the international business community, funding, information resources, minority- and women-outreach projects, partnerships with high schools, trade centers and institutes, and innovative instructional methods.

Foreign Students

Giammarella, M. "A Profile of the Foreign Student at a Public Two-Year College: The Borough of Manhattan Community College Response to the Financial Problems of Foreign Students." *Community Review,* 1986, 7 (1), 6–13.

This study examines enrollment trends among foreign college students and the financial problems faced by many. It considers the effects of the slow transfer of foreign exchange and inadequate and interrupted funds from home. Also described are Manhattan Community College's (New York) financial-aid programs, and financial-aid fraud and policies to discourage it.

Krasno, R. "The Contributions of the Community Colleges to International Education." Speech delivered at the Eighth Annual Conference on International Education, Lake Buena Vista, Fla., February 12–15, 1985. 23 pp. (ED 256 379)

This speech addresses the important role of community colleges in making a special contribution to international education. Because they have a high foreign-student population, community colleges have a key role to play in helping all U.S. schools think through the complex task of educating foreign students, integrating them into campus and community life, making certain that the curriculum is relevant to student needs, and ensuring that appropriate continuing education and lifelong learning opportunities exist for foreign students who have returned to their own countries.

Zikopoulos, M. (ed.). *Open Doors: 1987/88. Report on International Educational Exchange.* New York: Institute of International Education, 1987. 189 pp. (ED 303 117)

The 1987/88 edition of the Institute of International Education's annual publication on foreign student enrollments in the United States is presented. Foreign-student enrollments are broken down by college, country of origin, and academic and personal characteristics. The four parts of the report focus on the following: (1) the annual census of the distribution of foreign students in the United States in two- and four-year institutions and in public and private institutions, of institutions with most foreign students, and of foreign students by academic level, (2) cost-of-living expenditures by foreign students in the United States, and (3) intensive English-language programs. The report has eight appendices.

International Student Exchange

Bannon, S., and Kraemer, M. "In Someone Else's Shoes." *Community and Junior College Journal,* 1985, 55 (4), 39–40, 44–45.

This article describes a West German–American cultural exchange program, during which eighty-four German professionals studied at community colleges with appropriate curricula, participated in paid internships at local businesses, and stayed with a host family. Fifty U.S. community college students enjoyed a similar experience in Germany.

Fifield, M. L., and Sakamoto, C. M. (eds.). *The Next Challenge: Balancing International Competition and Cooperation.* Washington, D.C.: American Association of Community and Junior Colleges, 1987. 104 pp. (ED 280 548)

This collection of sixteen essays addresses various aspects of the role of community colleges in international relations and trade. Among the articles are "The Community College: An International Institution," by Wayne O'Sullivan, and "Building an International Agenda: An International Education Conference," by Julia Ribley and Clyde M. Sakamoto.

Hess, G. *Freshmen and Sophomores Abroad: Community Colleges and Overseas Academic Programs.* New York: Teachers College Press, 1982. 194 pp. (ED 231 467)

The mechanics of establishing and maintaining overseas academic programs are examined with respect to the community college level. The book includes chapters on the rationale for the involvement of community colleges in international programs, a model of community college involvement in overseas programming, and the impact of international programs on faculty and students.

Robinson, B. S. "New Dimensions in Intercultural Education at Community Colleges." Paper presented at the conference "Focus on the World: Meeting the Educational Challenge of the Future," Bridgewater, Mass., October 23–24, 1985. 9 pp. (ED 273 338)
The study describes efforts of community colleges in Massachusetts and other states to take up the challenge of intercultural education. Lansing Community College in Michigan provides one of the most dynamic study-abroad programs available in the nation, offering an opportunity for students to travel and study in Japan for nine months; the college also presents instruction in eight non-English languages. In Massachusetts, community college educators have participated in a national curriculum-development project designed to prepare intercultural modules for existing courses.

Ruth I. Cape is user services coordinator at the ERIC Clearinghouse for Junior Colleges.

Anita Y. Colby is associate director of the ERIC Clearinghouse for Junior Colleges.

INDEX

Abell, N., 21, 25
Adams, A. H., 110
African Studies Association, 7
Agency for International Development, U.S. (AID), 7, 82, 90, 105
Althen, G., 107
American Assembly, 25
American Association of Community and Junior Colleges (AACJC), 1, 3, 9, 10, 15, 57, 67, 72, 74, 80, 95. *See also* International/Intercultural Committee
American Association of State Colleges and Universities, 72, 74
American Council on Education, 15, 88, 97
American School of Guayaquil, 60
American Sociological Association, 20
American-Chinese Educational Consortium for Academic and Technical Exchange, 11
Anderson, C. J., 88, 98
Area-study centers, 7. *See also* International education
Armer, J. M., 20, 25
Arrival Program, YMCA, 91-93, 95
Art, teaching of, 19
Asian Studies Association, 7

Backman, E. L., 44
Bailey, T. A., 6, 15
Baldassare, M., 44, 107
Baliles, G. L., 14
Bannon, S., 116
Baran, E., 60
Barber, E., 44
Belize, and bilateral technical assistance programs, 82
Bergen Community College, 13, 71
Blanco, V., 71, 74
Bloom, A., 37, 44
Boyer, E. L., 67, 74
Brademas, J., 7
Breuder, R. L., 78, 84
Brevard Community College, 21, 68-70, 79, 82, 83
Brickman, W. W., 37, 44
Brigham Young University, 34, 41

Brookdale Community College, 60
Broome Community College, 22, 23
Broward Community College (BCC), 22, 59-61, 70
Brown, P. A., 112
Buenos Aires, American colleges in, 59
Burmeister-May, S., 114
Burn, B., 12, 15
Business community, and foreign-student involvement, 103. *See also* International business
Business training, 21, 70. *See also* Career training, International business

Campus activities, for foreign students, 91-92, 94
Career training, 11; for foreign students, 93; and study abroad, 30. *See also* Business training; Manpower training overseas; Technical assistance
Carnegie Council of Policy Studies, 12
Center for International Studies (CIS), 60
Central American Peace Scholarship Program, 82, 84
Channing, R. M., 71, 74
Chase, B., 21, 25
Classroom strategies. *See* Curriculum development, Teaching
Cleveland, H., 25
College Consortium for International Studies (CCIS), 11, 13, 47, 48, 50-53, 55
College Entrance Examination Board, 96, 98
Columbus International College (CIC), 59
Comenius, 14
Commission on the Future of Community Colleges, 1, 3
Community Colleges for International Development (CCID), 11, 13, 78-82
Community involvement, and foreign students, 91-92, 94, 99-100; funding for, 101-102; off-campus, 102-105; on-campus, 100-102; resources for, 106-107. *See also* Foreign students
Consortial projects, 10-11, 47, 48, 50-

119

National Governors' Association, 14, 16
Nielsen, N., 111
Nilles, M. F., 113
Nursing, teaching of, 21

Offices of international education, 100, 103. *See also* Foreign-student advisers; Program directors

Paquette, W., 113-114
Partnership in Service Learning, 11
Peace Corps, 7-8
People's Republic of China, 11
Perkins, J. A., 12, 16
Prast, L. L., 112
President's Commission on Foreign Languages and International Studies, 12, 16, 57, 64, 67, 75
Program directors, role of, 27, 28, 34, 35, 38, 72, 88. *See also* Foreign-student advisers; Offices of international education

Reichard, J., 62, 63, 64
Reischauer, H. O., 6
Republic of China (Taiwan), and bilateral technical assistance programs, 78, 80-81
Resources: on curriculum development, 112-114; for exchange faculty, 41-42; for foreign-student programs, 95-97, 115-116; on international business, 114-115; on international education, 110-112; for program development, 12-13, 72; for study-abroad programs, 34, 116-117; for technical assistance programs, 84
Rhinesmith, S., 107
Rhodes scholarship program, 37
Ribley, 70, 75
Robinson, B. S., 117
Rockland Community College, 8, 10
Romano, R., 22, 25
Rosenthal, A. A., 19, 25
Ross, M. G., 37, 44

Sakamoto, C. M., 13, 15, 44, 116
Salas, D. J., 114
Sam, D. F., 115
Scanlon, D., 5, 16
Schwartz, R., 20, 25
Sciences, teaching of, 20-21

Shannon, W. G., 1, 9-10, 22, 25
Silney, J., 61, 64
Singapore, American colleges in, 62
Singh, M., 83, 85
Smith, A. F., 18, 25
Smith-Mundt Act, 7
Social sciences, teaching of, 19-20
Southern Governors' Association, 14, 16
Spain, American colleges in, 59, 60
Speakers' bureaus, 104
State Department, U.S., 41
Stedman, J. B., 62, 65
Stewart, E. C., 44
Stewart, G., 107
Study-abroad programs, 1-2; 10, 11, 53; materials for, 34; nontraditional, 27-35, 53; orientation for, 33-34; promotion of, 28-32; and reentry, 34; resources on, 116-117; and selection of students, 32-33. *See also* Consortial projects
Surinam, Republic of, and bilateral technical assistance programs, 78-80
Switzerland, American colleges in, 59

Taiwan. *See* Republic of China
Tamarkin, T., 114
Task Force on International Education, 7, 16
Teaching, 17; in all disciplines, 18-22; and general education, 22-23, 72; materials for, 18, 24. *See also* Curriculum development; Faculty development; International education
Technical assistance, 7, 11, 77-79, 80; and community college outreach, 83-84; and Community Colleges for International Development, 78-82; future of, 84; and international business organizations, 82-83; and research grants, 97
Third-world countries, and Peace Corps, 7-8
Tillman, M., 98
Title VI-Foreign Studies and Language Development, 10
Tokyo-American Community College, 62
Tonkin, H., 26
Turkey, and bilateral technical assistance programs, 82-83
Two-year colleges. *See* International institutions

United Nations, 18. *See also* UNESCO
United Nations Educational, Scientific, and Cultural Organization (UNESCO), 5
U.S. Information Agency, 72, 75, 95, 102, 105, 106
University of Maryland, 19-20
University of Wisconsin, 28-29

Valencia Community College, 70-71
Vaughan, G. B., 67, 75

Visas: and exchange faculty, 40-41; and foreign students, 92
Volunteers, role of, 103, 106
Webster, S., 44
Welty, E., 32
Woolston, V., 90, 98
World Bank, 18, 83, 84

YMCA International Student Service (ISS), 91-93
Zikopoulos, M., 44, 58, 62, 65, 87, 98, 116

ORDERING INFORMATION

NEW DIRECTIONS FOR COMMUNITY COLLEGES is a series of paperback books that provides expert assistance to help community colleges meet the challenges of their distinctive and expanding educational mission. Books in the series are published quarterly in Fall, Winter, Spring, and Summer and are available for purchase by subscription as well as by single copy.

SUBSCRIPTIONS for 1990 cost $48.00 for individuals (a savings of 20 percent over single-copy prices) and $64.00 for institutions, agencies, and libraries. Please do not send institutional checks for personal subscriptions. Standing orders are accepted.

SINGLE COPIES cost $14.95 when payment accompanies order. (California, New Jersey, New York, and Washington, D.C., residents please include appropriate sales tax.) Billed orders will be charged postage and handling.

DISCOUNTS FOR QUANTITY ORDERS are available. Please write to the address below for information.

ALL ORDERS must include either the name of an individual or an official purchase order number. Please submit your order as follows:
  Subscriptions: specify series and year subscription is to begin
  Single copies: include individual title code (such as CC1)

MAIL ALL ORDERS TO:
  Jossey-Bass Inc., Publishers
  350 Sansome Street
  San Francisco, California 94104

OTHER TITLES AVAILABLE IN THE
NEW DIRECTIONS FOR COMMUNITY COLLEGES SERIES
Arthur M. Cohen, Editor-in-Chief
Florence B. Brawer, Associate Editor